Project Management Casebook

Instructors Manual

EDITORS

David I. Cleland,
Karen M. Bursic,
Richard Puerzer, and
A. Yaroslav Vlasak

Library of Congress Cataloging-in-Publication Data

Project management casebook. Instructor's manual / David I. Cleland
... [et al.].
    p.   cm.
  ISBN: 1-880410-18-4 (pbk.)
  1. Industrial project management--Case studies. I. Cleland, David I. II. Project Management Institute
HD69.P75P7283 1997
658.4'04--dc21   97-10752
                                                              CIP

Copyright © 1998 by the Project Management Institute. All rights reserved. Printed in the United States of America. No part of this work may be reproduced or transmitted in any form or by any means, electronic, manual, photocopying, recording, or by any information storage and retrieval system, without prior written permission of the publisher.

Book Team

Editor-in-Chief: James S. Pennypacker
Book Designer: Michelle Owen
Copyeditor: Toni D. Knott
Cover design by: James S. Pennypacker, Dewey Messer, and Michelle Owen
Production Coordinator: Mark S. Parker
Acquisitions Editor: Bobby R. Hensley

PMI books are available at special quantity discounts to use as premiums and sales promotions, or for use in corporate training programs. For more information, please write to the Business Manager, PMI Publishing Division, 40 Colonial Square, Sylva, NC 28779. Or contact your local bookstore.

The paper used in this book complies with the Permanent Paper Standard issued by the National Information Standards Organization (Z39.48—1984).

10 9 8 7 6 5 4 3 2 1

Project Management Casebook

Instructors Manual

Table of Contents

Chapter One: Planning   1

   The Benfield Column Repair Project   5

   Food Waste Composting at Larry's Markets   7

   Winning the Sydney to Hobart: A Case Study in Project Management   9

   Kodak's New Focus   11

   Managing Kuwait Oil Fields Reconstruction Projects   15

   Managing Resources and Communicating Results of Sydney's $7 Billion Clean Waterways Program   19

   Making Affordable Housing Attainable through Modern Project Management   23

   Goal Definition and Performance Indicators in Soft Projects: Building a Competitive Intelligence System   27

Chapter Two: Organizing   33

   Communicating Risk Management in Municipal Government Projects: City of New Orleans Computer-Aided Dispatch System Project   37

   Cape Town's Olympic Bid: A Race against the Clock   41

   Sydney 2000 Olympic Games: A Project Management Perspective   43

   Strategic Project Control Initiatives   47

   Libya: Redefining Challenge   51

   Land Reserve Modernization Project: The Future of Army Infrastructure   53

   R&D in the Insurance Industry: PM Makes the Difference   57

   Implementing Integrated Product Development: A Case Study of Bosma Machine and Tool Corporation   61

   How ICL Used Project Management Techniques to Introduce a New Product Range   65

Chapter Three: Motivating   69

   Communication Strategies for Major Public Works Projects: The Los Angeles Metro Rail Program under Siege   73

   Learning the Lessons of Apollo 13   75

   Taxol®: An Example of "Fast-Track" Drug Development   77

   Privatization in Patagonia: The Selling of Argentina's Largest Hydroelectric Plant   79

   Quesnel Air Terminal: Design/Build Works in the Public Sector   81

   The National Aero-Space Plane Program: A Revolutionary Concept   85

Chapter Four: Directing 91

Quality Management Works 95

Destroying the Old Hierarchies 97

Saturn's Vision for Program Management: A Different Kind of Approach 101

Using Project Management to Create an Entrepreneurial Environment in Czechoslovakia 105

The Channel Tunnel: Larger than Life, and Late 107

Minimizing Construction Claims under the Project Management Concept 111

Chapter Five: Controlling 115

Giving Mother Nature a Helping Hand 119

Managing Environmental Regulatory Approval Durations 121

Pittsburgh International Airport Midfield Terminal Energy Facility 125

Environmental Mega-Project under Way: Sludge Management in New York City 127

Gaining Project Acceptance 131

The Power of Politics: The Fourth Dimension of Managing the Large Public Project 135

The Environmental and Molecular Sciences Laboratory Project: Continuous Evolution in Leadership 139

Chrysler and Artemis: Striking Back with the Viper 141

St. Lucie Unit 2: A Nuclear Plant Built on Schedule 145

Measuring Successful Technical Performance: A Cost/Schedule/Technical Control System 149

The Legal Standards for "Prudent" Project Management 153

Chapter Six: General 157

Communicating Constraints: Schedule Baseline and Recovery Measures on the Hong Kong Airport Projects 161

Can We Talk?: Communications Management for the Waste Isolation Pilot Plant, a Complex Nuclear Waste Management Project 165

The Demise of the Superconducting Supercollider: Strong Politics or Weak Management 169

Boeing Spares Distribution Center: A World-Class Facility Achieved through Partnering 173

Responding to the Northridge Earthquake 177

A Town Makes History by Rising to New Heights 179

Real-World Challenges to a Multinational Project Team: Building a Manufacturing Facility in India 181

Total Quality Management and Project Management 185

Organization and Management of a Multi-Organizational Single Responsibility Project 189

Prudent and Reasonable Project Management 193

The Space Shuttle Challenger Incident 197

Appendix A: PMI's Code of Ethics for the Project Management Profession   201

Appendix B: Recommended Reading   203

Planning

1
PLANNING

The Benfield Column Repair Project   5

Food Waste Composting at Larry's Markets   7

Winning the Sydney to Hobart: A Case Study in Project Management   9

Kodak's New Focus   11

Managing Kuwait Oil Fields Reconstruction Projects   15

Managing Resources and Communicating Results of Sydney's $7 Billion Clean Waterways Program   19

Making Affordable Housing Attainable through Modern Project Management   23

Goal Definition and Performance Indicators in Soft Projects: Building a Competitive Intelligence System   27

1995 PMI International Project of the Year
The Benfield Column Repair Project

Ian Boggon, PMP, General Manager, INTENS SA

PM Network, February 1996, pp. 25–30

Synopsis

This case describes the Benfield Column Repair Project, the 1995 PMI International Project of the Year. The project was to quickly replace a large section of a regeneration column at a coal, chemical, and crude oil company in South Africa. The project required that a large number of resources be pooled from around the world to engineer the repairs to the regeneration column. All aspects of project management were utilized to accomplish the project. Thanks to excellent project management, plus creative solutions to a number of challenges, the project was completed ahead of schedule and under budget.

Learning Objectives

In discussing this case, students should gain a better understanding of:
- the use of a work breakdown structure
- the importance of building commitment from team members
- how special management methods can be used to aid a project
- that communications management is a key to a project
- how a large and complex project such as this can be very successful.

Discussion Questions and Possible Answers

1. A work breakdown structure (WBS) was used in the management of the project described in this case. According to the *PMBOK Guide*, what is the concept of the WBS?
   a. In the *PMBOK Guide*, section 5.3.3, Outputs From Scope Definition, a WBS is termed a deliverable-oriented grouping of project elements that organizes and defines the total scope of the project.
2. The WBS is also described as a key for the scope management of the project. Outline the process used in this project to develop the WBS.
   a. In the first meeting they used a brainstorming session with all interested parties present. Ideas were placed on post-it notes on a huge white board. At the second meeting, the WBS was refined and accepted. Times for each task were assigned by those who would carry out the tasks. This is essentially the same process documented in section 5.3.2, Tools and Techniques For Scope Definition, in the *PMBOK Guide*.

3. The author of this case presents communications management as "the golden thread which ran through the project." If the supplier relationships were less trustful, how would this have changed the management and success of the project?
    a. Because the supplier relationships enabled the suppliers to be trusted and relied upon, more effort was able to be put forth in expediting the project. Had the supplier relationships been less trustful, project managers would have had to have spent more time working with suppliers, assuring on time deliveries, and checking the quality of materials, and thus would not have been able to spend as much time expediting the project. Thus the project, although probably still a success, may not have been done as fast or as much under budget.
4. This project challenged the way in which things are usually done, and based its success on what were considered special management methods. Mention a couple of the examples from the project which you think reflect these "special" practices.
    a. Mutual trust through the use of verbal contracts, followed by written contracts later.
    b. One person is used to handle all purchase orders instead of a department. All orders were recorded in a diary.
    c. The only written reports to management were concerning costs and the schedule.
    d. The project team was located on-site and had a clear presence throughout the life of the project.
    e. The easy use of clear and proper communications.
    f. Credit given for work done ahead of schedule.
5. How did the project build commitment from every member of the team? List several reasons for this commitment.
    a. Scoreboard created to allow all to know project status and to recognize outstanding performance.
    b. Clear feedback for all involved (suppliers, management, etc.)
    c. The project team was located on-site and had a clear presence throughout the life of the project.
    d. Encouragement for enthusiasm and commitment was addressed from the inception of the project.
    e. A teamwork approach was taken as opposed to individual effort.

ADDITIONAL DISCUSSION POINTS:

The instructor may want to discuss the importance of the post-project analysis mentioned in the case as a source of continuous improvement in project management and as a part of continuous improvement in the company and its culture.

Food Waste Composting at Larry's Markets

Brant Rogers, Environmental Affairs Manager, Larry's Markets

PM Network, February 1995, pp. 32–33

Synopsis

This case describes a recycling project which is a part of an environmental program instituted by a chain of grocery stores. The project was a success in that it achieved its mission, pleasing customers and environmental agencies, as well as generating a profit. The case illustrates the wide applicability of project management.

Learning Objectives

During the discussion of and answering questions on this case, students will gain a better understanding of the following:
- the concept of a project's mission, vision, objectives, goals and strategies
- the applicability of project management to any size of project
- the wide range of project management applications
- when to use project management.

Discussion Questions and Possible Answers

1. The case description contains the following statement: "The project's mission was to capture all of the produce and floral department byproducts for composting by late 1993." The words mission, vision, objectives, and goals are very frequently used in management. What are their definitions and differences? Also, what were these for Larry's market project?

    a. From the book, *Project Management: Strategic Design and Implementation,* 2nd ed., by Cleland, Chapter 11, Project Planning, and from the book, *Strategic Management of Teams,* by Cleland, Chapter 1, The Concept and Process of Strategic Management, the following are defined:
    Vision: The vision is a dream or idea of what the future will hold. It is the general direction toward which an organization should head in order to be what its leaders want it to be.
    Mission: The organization's mission answers the basic question of "what business are we in?" It also offers a symbol around which all organizational effort is focused and provides the final performance criterion for a company.
    Objectives: Objectives are ongoing end purposes that will be achieved in the long run. Through the objectives, the mission is achieved. Objectives

can be used as a performance measure if stated with reference to quantitative or qualitative issues.

Goals: Goals are measurable milestones that will be achieved by the enterprise in the process of aiming toward the objectives. They are the basic components for developing a control process.

Strategies: Strategies are the design of the means through the allocation of resources.

2. Would this project be termed a success even if it meant no economic gain but the same environmental gain? If you were developing the proposal for this project given only the non-economic gain how would you "sell" it to stakeholders?

    a. Yes it would be a success given that environmental gain were at least one of the objectives of the project. However, the project would provide at least an indirect economic gain through public relations and as a morale booster through the company. Another of the objectives achieved was that the project also fulfilled a legal requirement on recycling rate.

3. This effort began as a project. In its current state, it is an ongoing effort by the company with no end in sight. Review the definition of a project and answer the following question: How can it be determined that an effort need no longer be managed as a project?

    a. From the *PMBOK Guide*, section 1.2, What Is a Project, a project is defined as "a temporary endeavor undertaken to create a unique product or service. Temporary means that every project has a definite beginning and a definite end. Unique means that the product or service is different in some distinguishing way from all similar products or services." Therefore, it could still be considered a project if it was designed to increase or change the company's recycling methods using a work breakdown structure and a schedule. However, once the recycling has been ingrained into the day-to-day business of the company in that it only needs to be monitored, it no longer requires management as a project.

4. The outcome of this project was outstanding. What do you think are the primary reasons for this success?

    a. The project had a clear mission and objectives from its origin.
    b. It serves as a source of pride and motivation to employees and customers.
    c. The project received recognition from the government and environmental groups that fostered commitment to the project.

ADDITIONAL DISCUSSION POINTS:

The instructor may want to have the students discuss how the methods and results for this project could be extended to a larger project. How do the challenges and the management of a project change with size?

Winning the Sydney to Hobart: A Case Study in Project Management

Lynn Crawford, University of Technology, Sydney

PMI *Proceedings*, 1993, pp. 53–59

SYNOPSIS

This case discusses the application of project management to the project of preparing for an ocean classic yacht race. The author makes specific reference to tasks which make up the project and relates them to specific work involved in project management. Campaigning for a yacht race includes determining the concept of the project (determine scope, risk assessment, review alternatives), developing the project (select the boat, establish the project team, prepare the boat), execute the project (procure the boat, train the team, enter the races) and finish the project (continually tune the boat, race the boat, and win). The case offers a novel look at project management in that the application is interesting and atypical.

LEARNING OBJECTIVES

Through the study of this case, students should gain a better understanding of:
- characteristics of a successful project
- the importance of all of the phases of a project
- the importance of a good project team
- the planning of a successful project
- the risk assessment of a project.

DISCUSSION QUESTIONS AND POSSIBLE ANSWERS

1. The project initiator believes that winning a yacht race depends 80 percent on the preparation stage and only 20 percent on the effort in the actual race. Einstein was quoted as saying that a creation is 10 percent inspiration and 90 percent perspiration. Which of these statements do you agree with? Why, given a project management context?

    a. The amount of planning for a project is very project dependent. The planning of a project is discussed in the *PMBOK Guide* in section 3.3.2, Planning Processes. It states that the planning of a project is very dependent on the previous experience in the area of the project, and should be commensurate with the scope of the project and the usefulness of the information developed. Einstein's 90 percent perspiration should include planning.

2. This project essentially describes a job-shop point of view. How might the creation of a fleet of championship boats change the described project life-cycle?

    a. The project life-cycle, described in *PMBOK Guide* in Section 2.1, made up of feasibility, planning and design, production, and turnover and start-up, would need to be refined to include more emphasis on the prototype and validation stages of development. Again, the question of 80 percent of the effort spent in planning would come into question as more work in production monitoring and performance may be required.

3. Cost management was described as subsidiary to time and quality objectives for this project. If this situation had been different, i.e., a restrictive boat budget, how might the project results have changed?

    a. It is difficult to say that the results would have changed at all. The experienced crew may have made the difference, and an inferior boat could have still been victorious. Likewise if the objective had truly been the enjoyment and pleasure of sailing as described in the case, the project would have been a success.

4. Had this same project analysis been performed on another boat in the Sydney to Hobart, how might it have pointed out any deficiencies in the project process?

    a. By benchmarking versus the *Assassin* project process, possible deficiencies in the process could be identified. For example, the funding differences or the lack of a "well-connected" project leader could have been a disadvantage of the less successful boat. Likewise, the amount of time spent on various aspects of the project could also be compared.

5. The case mentions the importance of meeting the requirements of five different certifications along with careful lobbying in order to enable entry of the yacht into the races. All projects face these kinds of challenges. Review the literature to develop your own model for dealing with these issues.

    a. These strategic issues need to be identified, assessed, and analyzed, and action should be taken in order to successfully deal with them. This is discussed by Cleland in *Project Management: Strategic Design and Implementation*, in the section on managing strategic project management issues. The use of such a cycle, assuring compliance to regulations and restrictions, for managing these strategic issues allows for the success of a project in the face of project restrictions and requirements.

ADDITIONAL DISCUSSION POINTS:

The case states: "Many project managers tackle their task without conscious reference to the various project management frameworks developed by theorists. This project was carried out by a project initiator with many years experience and a reputation in leading projects in the corporate and financial field. Application of a rigorous and systematic process to a project outside his normal field of activity was both instinctive and a major reason for the initiation of the project." Given this, have the students discuss the balance between managing by intuition and a project management framework.

Kodak's New Focus

Mark Maremont

Business Week, January 30, 1995, pp. 62–68

Synopsis

This case describes the strategic management change at Kodak and the subsequent changes in the company. The new CEO, George Fisher, wanted to make many changes at Kodak to keep the company competitive and powerful. These changes included: moving into new markets, selling off some businesses, developing new products, and changing the corporate culture. The case describes the project of making these changes and the challenges involved. It also describes management and the management of large projects from a corporate perspective.

Learning Objectives

Through the study of this case and the discussion questions, students should gain a better understanding of:
- the importance of recognizing a corporation's culture
- the challenges of a change in leadership
- the importance of a mission and clear vision when taking on a project
- the differences in management style
- the strategic management of an enterprise.

Discussion Questions and Possible Answers

1. Since George Fisher was named as the new CEO of Kodak in 1993, many changes have taken place. Is there any resemblance between a new administration taking over a company and the undertaking of a new project?

    a. *PMBOK Guide's* description of a project is: "A temporary undertaking to create a unique product or service." From this perspective, a new administration with new goals and with the desire of transforming a company is undertaking the project of trying to create a new organization. Thus, the transformation of a company by new leadership could in fact be considered a project.

2. Many symptoms of poor management can be identified from the case including large debt, slow decision-making, multiple reorganizations, avoidance of risk taking, disjointed efforts, etc. However, what was the real problem Kodak was facing before 1993?

a. Projects are the building blocks of the future of a company. Kodak had compromised itself with a wide range of business interests. They were not capturing the market for several of their research projects, due mainly to their lack of marketing orientation.
   b. The cultural and hierarchical matrix organization prevented Kodak from moving into new markets. The non-accountable management style found in its culture, with no true feedback mechanisms, also discouraged motivation.
3. New Kodak CEO George Fisher is described as taking a slow approach to reorganizing Kodak. He claims that he is doing this in order to preserve Kodak's successful business segments. By doing this, the scope of the reorganization effort is controlled and focused. Draw comparisons between this method of change and *PMBOK Guide's* section 5, Project Scope Management.
   a. In *PMBOK Guide*, section 5, project scope management is described as the process required to ensure that projects include all work required and only the work required. By focusing on Kodak's less successful business segments, especially research and development, and not needlessly pressuring their successful business segments, Kodak is keeping the turnaround of the project in proper focus.
4. How are the use of Kodak's new measures concerning project progression and completion going to affect these projects and their management? What are some of the intangible or cultural effects? What guidelines can be used to ensure that this is done effectively?
   a. The projects will be run more strictly, with defined schedules, causing more concentration on the bottom line. The intangible or cultural effects may be that the company in general will also be run more strictly. All of the methods within the company will change, with an effort to become more lean as a company.
   b. Guidelines concerning this project time management are included in *PMBOK Guide,* section 6. For instance, by viewing the project as a series of tasks with associated predicted duration, project schedules can be developed allowing project managers to adhere to a standard.
5. Kodak has obviously had many successful projects, but are described as bad at developing products aimed at the less costly consumer market. How might its project management be focused to address these markets?
   a. By focusing on scope management and improving the initial focus of a project, it is easier to assure that the final developed project will meet the desired characteristics, especially in terms of market desires. Guidelines regarding this can be found in *PMBOK Guide*, section 5, Project Scope Management. These guidelines will cover such areas as scope change control, which assures that changes are beneficial and that those changes are facilitated as they occur.
6. Fisher's managerial style is described as rather informal, resembling that of a coach or parent. How do you feel about this type of leader?

a. In *Successful Project Managers: Leading Your Team to Success* by Jeffrey Pinto and O. P. Kharbanda, ten keys to leadership are listed: show the way, have a compass, give due credit, take risks, keep faith, act the part, delegate, be enthusiastic, be competent, and thrive on change. Fisher seems to be embracing several of these characteristics, especially giving due credit and acting enthusiastic. Again, this style may not always be the most effective, but in a well-established, successful company pursing change, it may well be the best method.

ADDITIONAL DISCUSSION POINTS:

Kodak's new focus can be stated as: Quality, customer needs, and shorter product development to reduce costs and create a more dynamic corporate culture. How could Kodak CEO Fisher find some of the project management principles such as the use of interdisciplinary teams helpful in this endeavor?

Managing Kuwait Oil Fields Reconstruction Projects

Mehdi Adib, Bechtel Corporation

PMI Canada *Proceedings*, 1994, pp. 184–90

Synopsis

This case describes the project of reconstructing the Kuwait Oil Company's oil fields following the Gulf War in 1991. The project was conceived in November 1990, before the Gulf War even began, and ended in June 1993. The case describes many of the challenges the project faced including the need for basic necessities (water, shelter, etc.), the organization of the project, and the various aspects of managing the project. The project ended a success, with all of the oil wells repaired, a huge amount of oil reclaimed, and production goals as desired. This case shows the importance of planning and the use of creative solutions to project challenges.

Learning Objectives

Through the study of this case and the associated discussion questions, students should gain a better understanding of:
- the management of a large project
- the importance of project schedule management
- the importance of infrastructure in a large project
- the challenges of managing a multinational multicultural project.

Discussion Questions and Possible Answers

1. This project was a major undertaking. The challenges it faced ranged from providing the basics for being able to live in the desert (water and shelter) to finding creative methods for getting imports into the country through non-traditional routes. From the author's point of view, the project went rather smoothly. To which factors do you attribute the success of this project?

    a. Planning—Planning for this project began in November 1990, well before the Gulf war and the implementation of the project on March 4, 1991.

    b. Financial Resources—The author does not mention financial resources; however, knowing the importance of the oil reserves of Kuwait and the wealth of the country, one may easily infer that the project did not face economic restrictions.

c. Adequate Project Management—The planning process, the close relationship between engineering and construction teams, and the use of tools such as a work breakdown structure exemplify the use of project management.
   d. The clear and attainable mission of the project.
2. This case describes an enormous undertaking made up of many different projects. Which of these projects can be considered the most important? Why?
   a. The most important projects can be broken into two groups:
      1. Those which must be accomplished chronologically before the others because the others are dependent on their completion. These include such projects as: extinguishing the well fires, and eliminating the risk of unexploded shells and mines.
      2. Those which create the necessary infrastructure to accomplish the project as a whole such as the creation and distribution of housing, food, and water. Before any large-scale work on the recovery of the oil resources can begin, there must be the support for those accomplishing this work.
3. One of the regular outputs of the development of the project plan is the work breakdown structure. Define the work breakdown structure and its benefits.
   a. The *PMBOK Guide* defines the work breakdown structure in section 5.3.3, Outputs of Scope Definition. It states that: "A work breakdown structure is a deliverable oriented grouping of project elements that organizes and defines the total scope of the project: work not in the work breakdown structure is outside of the scope of the project." It continues: "Each descending level represents an increasingly detailed definition of a project component. Project components may be products or services."
   b. In *Project Management: Strategic Design and Implementation* by Cleland, 2nd ed., Chapter 11, Project Planning, the work breakdown structure is defined as that which: "divides the overall project into work elements that represent singular work units, assigned either with the organization or to an outside organization such as a vendor."
   Some of the uses for a work breakdown structure are:
   - summarizing all products and services comprising the project, including support and other tasks
   - displaying the interrelationships of the work packages to each other, to the total project, and to other engineering activities in the organization
   - establishing the authority-responsibility matrix organization
   - estimating project cost
   - performing risk analysis
   - scheduling work packages
   - developing information for managing the project
   - providing a basis for controlling the application of resources on the project
   - providing reference points for getting people committed to support the project.

4. How were the multinational relationships handled in this project?
   a. Tasks were "tailor made" to suit a team available to handle that project. These teams thus were led and made up of members able to communicate with each other. Guidelines for these issues can be found in *PMBOK Guide*, section 9, Project Human Relations Management, and *PMBOK Guide*, section 10, Project Communications Management. These sections describe how these issues can be focused upon and successfully managed.
5. This project was handled by the Bechtel Corporation, a private company, and not the Kuwaiti government. List some of the advantages to this project being handled privately and not publicly.
   a. Experience—Bechtel knew how to handle the various jobs
   b. Multinational hiring ability—able to create the necessary work force
   c. Cost and scheduling controls
   d. Bechtel's existing resources and its ability to import resources to cover project necessities.
   e. Ability to plan the project before it began (the Kuwaiti government was concerned with much more pressing matters)
6. Figure 1 shows the organization chart of the Al-Tameer project. What kind of organization does this represent?
   a. The organization chart resembles a functional organization. However, the purpose of the whole organization is this single project. Therefore, each of the functions can be taken as subcomponents of the project and thus the chart might describe a project organization.

ADDITIONAL DISCUSSION POINTS:

The financial aspects of this project, although rarely mentioned in the case, obviously had an effect on how the project was carried out. Discuss how you believe finances may have driven the project, may have constrained the project, and may otherwise have affected the project.

Managing Resources and Communicating Results of Sydney's $7 Billion Clean Waterways Program

Larry Johnson, Consultant to the Sydney Water Board's Clean Waterways Program
Richard Wankmuller, Consultant to the Sydney Water Board's Clean Waterways Program

PMI *Proceedings*, 1992, pp. 127–33

Synopsis

This case describes the management of a group of projects oriented to clean up the Sydney beaches and waterways within twenty years. The Government of New South Wales and the Sydney Water Board committed $7 billion (1991 $Aus) to the endeavor. The authors describe in detail the control systems used in the project, the assignment of resources among competing projects, and internal and external communications. The case also depicts and explain some of the reports used in the project.

Learning Objectives

Through the study of the case, the students will gain a better understanding of:
- the differences between mission, objectives and goals
- performance reporting
- project control
- challenges of governmental projects.

Discussion Questions and Possible Answers

1. The case presents three of the reports used to control the project's development. Section 10.3 of the *PMBOK Guide*, Performance Reporting, lists the elements that a performance report should include. Evaluate the detailed schedule report depicted in Figure 2 using the *PMBOK Guide* guidelines.

    a. According to *PMBOK Guide*, section 10.3, "performance reporting should generally provide information on scope, schedule, cost and quality. Many projects also require information on risk and procurement." The elements are: scope, schedule, cost, quality, risk, and procurement.
    Scope: The report references the tasks being developed. From the information available in the case, the tasks should be more specific or the report should come with a clear task descriptor.
    Schedule: The report clearly addresses this element.
    Cost: The report covers this element.

Quality, Risk, and Procurement: It is not clear from the case whether or not these elements have been considered.
2. The case mentions the difficulties of scheduling and budgeting due to out of scope activities and poor estimates of baseline schedule duration and budgets. How should the project manager control the undertaking of activities which are out of the project's scope?
   a. The project manager is responsible for the entire operation of the project and should use work breakdown structure, performance reports, and scope management plans to control the proper use of resources (see section 5.5, Scope Change Control, *PMBOK Guide*).
3. Define and highlight the differences between a project's mission, objectives, and goals and provide examples from the case.

   Mission—Describes a broad "vision" of the business the organization or the project is pursuing. Example from case: Upgrade the sewage treatment plants.

   Objectives—Desired future position of the project in terms of cost, schedule, or technical performance (aimed at achieving the project's mission). Example from the case: Develop standard operating procedures at the sewage treatment plants.

   Goals—Measurable (in terms of time) milestones (aimed at achieving project objectives). Example from the case: Deliver the final standard operating procedure for influent screens at North Head Sewage Treatment Plant by April 1, 1992.
4. Define what is meant by a "media plan" and list elements that should be contained within it. Discuss the importance of good external communications.
   a. A media plan (as described in this case) is simply a method for external communication to gain public support and promote public participation in the project. It was a way to generate two-way communications and solicit public input into the project.
   b. The media plan should contain a strategy for directing and responding to media inquiries and a clear communications policy detailing who acts as a focal point for dealing with the press and what they are permitted to divulge.
   c. When the public is a significant stakeholder in a project, as in this case, it is absolutely necessary to have policies and procedures for informing them of the progress of the project.
   d. The instructor may also wish to provide examples of companies that either successfully or unsuccessfully dealt with the media in various situations. For example, when the makers of Tylenol were faced with tampering, they effectively informed the public about their plans for removing Tylenol from the store shelves and creating new tamper-proof packaging.
5. Is the one-page summary schedule report shown in Figure 4 an effective means of communication?
   a. It depends on where the report is sent. In the case, they state that the report is for managers and is used in staff meetings. The report is probably adequate for this purpose but may not be for the project manager or engineer.
   b. The report is also very "busy" and somewhat difficult to interpret.

ADDITIONAL DISCUSSION POINTS:

The students can work in teams to identify the elements and processes necessary to control a project.

Chapter 13, Project Control, of *Project Management: Strategic Design and Implementation*, 2nd ed., by D. Cleland, states the following: "Control is the process of monitoring, evaluating, and comparing planned results with actual results to determine the status of the project cost, schedule, and technical performance objectives." The process proposed by Cleland is a non-ending cycle of: establishing standards, observing performance, comparing actual performance, and taking corrective actions.

Making Affordable Housing Attainable through Modern Project Management

Paul L. Berg, Enterprise Builders, Inc.

PM Network, August 1994, pp. 12–18

Synopsis

This case illustrates how project management can contribute to achieving the social objective of local governments through an affordable housing project. The author describes some of the innovative ways the project management developed to work with stakeholders, how adequate communications help to reduce costs, the key superintendent characteristics, and guidelines on job site safety. This project was successfully finished and has fostered the development of a similar endeavor.

Learning Objectives

From this affordable housing project, the students will acquire a better understanding of:
- leadership skills
- activity duration estimation
- project scope
- teams.

Discussion Questions and Possible Answers

1. The author identifies some of the most important skills or abilities of a superintendent that help to keep a project on track. Which are those? Can you add some?

    a. The author identifies the following common traits:
    - "A seasoned, working knowledge of construction details accumulated over the years from a variety of construction projects.
    - An attitude of approaching each project as an unique opportunity to become better educated in the intricacies of the subtrades. The best superintendents ask, listen, and discuss rather than tell and yell!
    - The ability to plan overall objectives to achieve specific milestones along the way and organize them into short-term goals for each trade.
    - The ability to effectively communicate and discuss the plan in weekly coordination meetings to set assertive goals and work out objectives so that the goals can be met.

- The habit of walking around daily to follow-up personally on the accomplishment of tasks, goals, and schedules. Effective follow-up helps to put a supervisor in control.
- The ability to regularly review achievements and identify new problems at weekly meetings, which is a result of planning, communicating, and controlling—in that order."
  b. Other leadership skills cited in the literature include: personal ambition; visibility to employees; available to listen, debate, and gather facts; decisive; see the best in people; avoid making things complex; fair and patient; work hard; understand the technology; good interpersonal skills; understand the management process; and the ability to see the systems and strategic context of the project (adapted from Cleland, David I., *Project Management: Strategic Design and Implementation*, 2nd ed., Chapter 16, Project Leadership).

2. The case stresses the importance of planning as crucial to the success of the project. During the planning phase of a project it is necessary to develop a strategy that addresses all the issues that can influence the project. What are the topics that the planning strategy should cover?
   a. P.W.G. Morris on, *The Management of Projects*, Chapter 8, The Management of Projects: The New Model, as paraphrased, states that the following topics should typically be covered:
      - clear identification of the project objectives, and how those are going to be achieved
      - strategy and environment analysis
      - safety and quality policies
      - role of the project actors: sponsor, owner, vendors, consultants, etc.
      - financial objectives, funding, and cost analysis
      - design, technical, and logistic approach
      - work breakdown and work package structure
      - check-up points
      - legal, insurance, employment, information systems, communications (in and out) and technological issues.

3. The project team put special effort into the fulfillment of the schedule so the tenants would be able to move on the predetermined dates. Therefore time durations were crucial for the completion of this goal. What are the techniques more frequently used to estimate activity duration?
   a. *PMBOK Guide*, Section 6.3.2, Tools and Techniques for Activity Duration Estimating, identifies the following three methods:
      - "Expert Judgment: This expertise may be provided by a group or an individual with specialized knowledge or training. Durations are often difficult to estimate because of the number of factors which can influence them (e.g., resource levels, resource productivity). Expert judgment guided by historical information should be used whenever possible. If such expertise is not available, the estimates are inherently uncertain and risky.
      - Analogous Estimating. Analogous estimating, also called top-down estimating, means using the actual duration of a previous, similar activity as the basis for the estimate project duration of a future activity. It is frequently used to estimate project duration when there is a

limited amount of detailed information about the project. Analogous estimating is a form of expert judgment.
- Simulation. Simulation involves calculating multiple durations with different sets of assumptions. The most common is Monte Carlo Analysis in which a distribution of probable results is defined for each activity and used to calculate a distribution of probable results for the total project."

4. What two or three scope management factors were most critical to the success of this project? Why?

   a. Early on, the project team established clear lines of communication and defined roles and agreed that the schedule must be rigorously adhered to. The scope of the project was well defined before ground was broken. The CPM schedule was updated as needed and provided data from the first building to search for ways to save time throughout the rest of the project. The scope of the project called for the use of materials that were attractive yet met cost, delivery, constructability, and quality criteria. Good communication between subcontractors made transitions between them easier.

ADDITIONAL DISCUSSION POINTS:

Scope Statement Exercise. According to *PMBOK Guide* a well-written scope statement is essential for effective scope management. The scope statement should contain three parts: project justification, project deliverables, and project objectives. Assign students to groups of three to five and present them with a hypothetical project. Then ask them to develop a scope statement for the project.

See Duncan, W. R., Scoping Out a Scope Statement, *PM Network*, December, 1994, pp. 47–48, for additional guidelines on writing a scope statement.

Goal Definition and Performance Indicators in Soft Projects: Building a Competitive Intelligence System

François Lacasse, Université du Québec à Hull

PMI Canada *Proceedings*, 1986, pp. 247–52

Synopsis

This case discusses the setting up of a competitive intelligence system (CIS) in an agency of government. Specifically, the case presents an informal project management approach that initially failed, but was later revised to enable the project to be successfully implemented. The case uses a lessons learned format to describe what was done and why it did not work. Originally, the CIS project data idea was the result of a complete review and strategic reorientation which started in 1984. At that time, management believed that such a system could provide valuable information on Canada's chief competitors for tourist dollars in markets identified as being the most promising. This intelligence was to provide a continual monitoring of how Canadian destinations were likely to perform compared to other destinations and also provide early identification of threats and opportunities in this sector.

Learning Objectives

The students will learn the importance of adequate planning, including the evaluation of all key assumptions, when trying to successfully accomplish a project. When discussing this case, the following points should be addressed:
- the importance of having goals logically flow from an organization's mission and objectives
- the need to establish specific targets or milestones that will lead to the successful attainment of goals
- some of the problems that may develop when the above guidelines are not properly followed
- the problems that are associated with an informal or loosely planned implementation strategy
- some of the important factors that play a crucial role in the success of a project.

DISCUSSION QUESTIONS AND POSSIBLE ANSWERS

1. Describe some of the scope management problems created by trying to use one goal statement as the sole guiding factor on the project in this case. Define scope management for any project.

    a. The original goal was to have a CIS that was at least as good as the best system existing in the private sector completely operational within two years. Although the case does mention that the need for a CIS was identified in a strategic orientation, it is still unclear how this goal ties into the overall strategy and mission of the agency. In fact, one may question whether or not it is truly a goal at all. Traditionally, goals can be thought of as specific steps that lead to the accomplishment of organizational objectives. This further emphasizes the link between objectives and goals. Without these guiding features, this goal turned out to be rather vague and unusable. Before trying to develop an action plan, specific milestones (or short-range goals) must be developed that will lead to the successful accomplishment of the overall goals.

    b. *PMBOK Guide* Chapter 5, Project Scope Management, states that: "Project Scope Management includes the processes required to ensure that the project includes all the work required, and only the work required, to complete the project successfully. It is primarily concerned with defining and controlling what is or is not included in the project."

2. Briefly describe how the original project management team(s) were organized. Identify some of the problems resulting from trying to operate under this structure.

    a. The project management structure was under the head of research and planning and was to be performed by two teams, one internal to the organization and the other external (composed of consultants). Under this two-team approach, there appeared to be little cooperative effort. While the internal team was reorganizing the data that would eventually be used by the system, the consultants were trying to devise and design a system that met the quality and completeness standard of the best business practices. There appeared to be no communication between the internal group and external group as to what type of system was actually needed. This was partly a result of the vague sense of project direction. For example, the following questions were never even considered: Did the organization really need the best available business standard? How was it going to access the performance of the consultants with this vague standard?

    b. Although the two teams met every other week, the case gives the impression that there was no valuable exchange of information and little cooperation between the teams. A key contributing factor was the establishment of work assignments, with no provision for interfacing with the other group to obtain valuable feedback. Another contributing factor to these circumstances was the way that the implementation and planning phases were being accomplished simultaneously. Without adequate up-front planning, the implementation strategy would have to be accomplished haphazardly.

3. What were some of the specific problems that were originally encountered by the project teams?
    a. Since no attempt was made to get input from the eventual system users, serious organizational resistance was encountered. As a result, there was a general lack of interest among the potential CIS users. Relying on the "best system available" criteria proved to be impractical and infeasible. Contrary to one of their key assumptions, no one single dominant private model of a CIS existed. Each organization had modeled its system to fit its particular strategic needs. There was no real objective or goal that could serve to guide the team toward one direction. As previously discussed, the goal it had was too vague to be of practical use to the team. As stated in the case, the project had been inadequately planned. The company basically treated the project like a routine procurement purchase that did not warrant any additional planning.
    b. No attempt had been made to devise a WBS, so that there were no work packages to be assigned. The necessary steps to reorient the culture to using such a system were never undertaken. The potential system users were never consulted for their advice on how to implement these procedures. Consequently, the operational plans were never revised to incorporate the daily operations of the new CIS.
4. What were the keys to project success as cited in the case? What other factors influence the success or failure of a project?
    a. The factors identified in the case are:
        - Design the system so as to satisfy the needs of the lower levels.
        - The system should be designed and perceived to allow improvements in job performance that are followed by future rewards and recognition.
        - The case also cites the need to have the system inspired by the "best business practices," and not to fit the organization's culture by mandate. However, it seems that the system should be based on an organization's needs and fit into its strategic planning processes.
        - The people who would have to run and use the system need to feel a sense of project ownership.
    b. O. Kharbanda and J. Pinto in *Successful Project Managers: Leading Your Team to Success*, Chapter 4, Project Critical Success Factors, identify the following critical success factors, as paraphrased:
        - project mission—with clear goals and objectives
        - top management support—the support required to carried out the implementation (resources, authority)
        - schedule plan—a clear definition of each activity and stage in a time frame
        - client consultation—with the final user of the project, to gain acceptance and feedback
        - personnel—the search, selection, hiring, and training of the right project team members
        - technical tasks—the technological proficiency required to carry out each project activity
        - client acceptance—the final approval and acceptance from the intended users
        - monitoring and feedback—the control system that guarantees the adequate revision in each activity and stage

- communication—the process of gathering, processing, and distributing all relevant information
- troubleshooting—the ability of making the right decisions when the unexpected happens.

From a research project that that looked at over 400 projects and tried to assess the importance of the ten factors, Pinto and Slevin identified the mission as the most important factor in the study.

5. Describe the eventual implementation strategy used on this project. What are some of the potential problems of this approach?

   a. The implementation strategy called for a competitive atmosphere in which the overall project was divided into a series of mini-projects to be executed by small teams of volunteers within the organization. Basically, the agency provided the necessary guidelines, money, and technical support along with a means to evaluate these mini-projects. In addition, management decided to keep the specialized CIS staff to a minimum. The bulk of the work was to be accomplished by the line personnel through this informal team process. These teams of volunteers would submit a short project proposal to the CIS team and, if approved, would assume responsibility for running the monitoring system. Overall, the approach taken by management seemed to lack a firm sense of direction.

   b. The student may also care to elaborate on some of the more detailed aspects of this informal approach. In essence, the agency seemed to be backing off from its original position of having a system operational within two years. Instead of using a more formal and planned project management approach to establish this system, the organization is now trying to install this system through an informal type of task force approach. Although the case gives the impression that each mini-project was adequately controlled while instilling ownership in the employees, there still lacked an overall plan to tie everything together. The overall approach seemed to be haphazard in nature. In short, the project was lacking an unifying goal that tied all efforts together.

   c. One can also argue that this volunteer task force approach in effect deemphasized the importance of the project. For such an encompassing project, it seems unlikely that this ad hoc approach would truly be successful. The establishment of mini-projects could be better accomplished by first establishing a WBS and then assigning the resulting work packages to the best qualified individuals. There appears to be no clear link between the work that needs to be done and what the various task forces submit as proposals.

ADDITIONAL DISCUSSION POINTS:

The instructor may be interested in discussing why this very informal approach to project management was successful in this particular case. Furthermore, the instructor may want to address the question of why these small task teams consisting of volunteers proved to be so successful in this environment. Finally, the instructor may want to discuss the author's implication that software projects warrant the use and application of special project management techniques.

ORGANIZING

2
ORGANIZING

Communicating Risk Management in Municipal Government Projects: City of New Orleans Computer-Aided Dispatch System Project   37

Cape Town's Olympic Bid: A Race against the Clock   41

Sydney 2000 Olympic Games: A Project Management Perspective   43

Strategic Project Control Initiatives   47

Libya: Redefining Challenge   51

Land Reserve Modernization Project: The Future of Army Infrastructure   55

R&D in the Insurance Industry: PM Makes the Difference   57

Implementing Integrated Product Development: A Case Study of Bosma Machine and Tool Corporation   61

How ICL Used Project Management Techniques to Introduce a New Product Range   65

Communication Risk Management in Municipal Government Projects: City of New Orleans Computer-Aided Dispatch System Project

Michael Newell, Orleans Parish Communication District

PMI *Proceedings*, 1995, pp. 224–33

Synopsis

This case describes the purchasing and implementation process of an upgrade of a 911 emergency phone service in the city of New Orleans. Through the case, the author presents the communication and authority challenges faced by a project manager when dealing with powerful and independent stakeholders such as the fire, police, and emergency medical departments. The case provides a general but complete description of a 911 service and illustrates the previous service used in the city of New Orleans as well as an initial unsuccessful renovation attempt. The case also presents a creative alternative for vendor/implementor selection to the common bidding process. Finally, the case discusses the formal and informal communication challenges faced by this type of complex project.

Learning Objectives

In reviewing this case, the students will learn the importance of formal and informal communications of a project. They will also become familiar with a RFP purchasing process. After discussing the case, the students should gain a better understanding of:
- communication challenges with stakeholders (government departments, vendors, project owners)
- dealing with project team members not under the authority of the project manager
- learning from a previous project failure
- handling governmental organizations and budgetary restrictions
- the key skills of a project manager.

Discussion Questions and Possible Answers

1. The *PMBOK Guide*, section 2.4, Key General Management Skills, describes the most important personal tools of a project manager. Which of these

skills do you think were the most valuable in the project management of this project?

   a. All five of the key skills are valuable to a project manager: leading, communicating, negotiating, problem solving, and influencing the organization. It is possible that the student may perceive communicating and problem solving as the most important skills for this project. However, for the smooth development of any project, a good combination of all of the skills is important.

2. The *PMBOK Guide*, section 10, Project Communication Management, analyzes a project's communications process in four main phases. List communication challenges the project faced and classify these challenges in the different phases.

   a. The geographic distance between team members. Section 10.1, Communications Planning, and Section 10.2, Distribution.
   b. The lack of authority of the project manager over team members. Section 10.1, Communications Planning.
   c. Preconceived notions between departments about their parts in the process and their working conditions. Section 10.1, Communications Planning.
   d. The need for strict adherence to the RFP proposal evaluation process. Section 10.3, Performance Reporting.

3. What was the project manager's main challenge in completing the project?

   a. The project manager had no clear authority over the managers of the project team. He had to gain their trust by becoming a facilitator, not an appointed leader.
   b. The project had already been attempted and failed. This failure served as a barrier to the success of the project, despite the use of project management in the second effort.
   c. There were geographical distances between project team members requiring the use of communication methods other than face to face meetings and discussions.
   d. There was competition between project team members creating differences in their requirements for a successful outcome of the project.
   e. The necessity of using the RFP method for evaluating the vendor's proposals instead of the traditional bidding methods.

4. Explain the difficulties of managing a project involving stakeholders with different objectives in the project, i.e., the relationship between the vendor and customer.

   a. In this case, the failure of the first system was due to these differing objectives. In the second effort, the project manager used the RFP proposal evaluation method as well as a defined and monitored working relationship between the vendor and the customer to assure that both party's objectives would be acceptable.

5. Would the standardization of the procurement methods described in the case serve the city well in the future? Would you recommend that project

managers be required for similar tasks in the future? Where do you draw the line on the necessity of using project management?

a. The RFP method is useful for such large software and hardware projects with outside vendors. It would be management overkill to use this method for simpler tasks such as regular procurement processes. Thus, it could be required for very large and complex projects. Likewise, project management need not be used for day-to-day tasks which are considered under the regular scope of business. It is necessary for ad hoc undertakings.

ADDITIONAL DISCUSSION POINTS:

The instructor may want to divide the class into two teams and organize a debate on the following statement: "One of the deciding issues in the interviewing process was my conviction that the project management methodology could be applied to any type of project and the project manager need not have experience in the area directly as long as this is done. This was important since there are very few people available who have experience in this area."

Cape Town's Olympic Bid: A Race against the Clock

Project Pro, March 1996, pp. 7–10

SYNOPSIS

This case describes the use of project management in the development of a bid for Capetown, South Africa, to become the host for the 2004 Olympic Games. Project management is used in order to effectively manage the scope, communications, and other important components necessary in the development of the bid. This case describes some of the specific tools used for this unusual project.

LEARNING OBJECTIVES

Through the study of this case, students should gain a better understanding of:
- the wide range of project management applications
- the importance of project cost management
- the steps involved in developing an Olympic bid
- the stakeholder management involved in developing sponsorship for the Olympics.

DISCUSSION QUESTIONS AND POSSIBLE ANSWERS

1. Although the Olympics are an entertainment and sporting event, they are very much tied with financial performance. As a project manager, what are the main steps in assuring proper project cost management, and assuring economic success?

    a. The *PMBOK Guide,* section 7, Project Cost Management, is made of four main sections covering the main processes of project cost management. These four steps are: resource planning, cost estimating, cost budgeting, and cost control. Through managing using these steps, project managers will minimize the risk of running into economic trouble.

2. Obviously, hosting the Olympic Games could be economically beneficial to Capetown. Given this, how much of a risk is the investment in preparing the bid? How would the efforts completed to create the bid document be best used to aid the city if Cape Town is not awarded as the host city of the 2004 Olympic games?

    a. The risk in the creation of the document is necessary for the process of being selected as a host city. From a risk management perspective, it would be wise to publicize that the effort and cost involved in creating the bid will be less of a burden if the bid document can be used for other means. For example, the document will assess the weaknesses and strengths in the city and identify potential improvements in its infrastructure. However, the main objective of the document and the project is to be named host for the Olympics.

3. Benchmarking can be used in this project, i.e., matching Atlanta's preparation effort. How can this be beneficial in the management of the project?

   a. Risks in the project in terms of scope, economics, etc., can be more readily identified and prepared for when benchmarking the project. Additionally, the scale of the effort required to create the bid is known, allowing for more accurate planning by the project management team.

4. This case was written in 1996. If possible, update the results of the bidding process for the 2004 Olympic Games, focusing on South Africa's bid. From your research, what were the strengths and/or weaknesses responsible for the success/failure of its bid?

   a. Chances are, the success or failure of this project will depend on all of the following: politics, communications, resources, and the effective use of project management. A student's answer could describe any or all of these factors.

5. In the case, Mr. Gundlach describes his task as "to catch all of the activities we have to perform." Do you see this description as having any resemblance to a project management endeavor?

   a. This quote sounds like the definition of a work breakdown structure, capturing who, when, milestones, and communication paths.
   b. Mr. Gundlach is essentially serving as a project manager, managing time, resources, meeting deadlines, etc.

6. A WBS is the backbone of the project management of any project. According to the *PMBOK Guide*, what is the concept of the work breakdown structure? Do you see any resemblance between the work done in developing the Olympic bid and the WBS?

   a. In the *PMBOK Guide*, section 5.3.3, Outputs From Scope Definition, a work breakdown structure is a deliverable-oriented grouping of project elements that organizes and defines the total scope of the project.
   b. The quote: "catching all of the activities to be performed" mentioned in Question 4 sounds like one of the steps in the development of a work breakdown structure.

ADDITIONAL DISCUSSION POINTS:

The instructor may want to use the following question for discussion: If the closest major city to you were considering an Olympic bid, what would be the five main challenges that city would face?

The instructor may have the students research the Los Angeles and Barcelona games as well as World Cup preparations in order to determine the challenges these cities and countries faced in preparing for these undertakings.

Sydney 2000 Olympic Games: A Project Management Perspective

David Eager, University of Technology, Sydney

PMI *Proceedings*, 1997, pp. 227–31

Synopsis

This case describes the Sydney 2000 Olympic Games from a project management perspective. The Sydney 2000 Olympic Games is a large-scale and very complex project involving a diverse range of activities and large numbers of people. Given the nature and vast scale of this project, sound and exemplary project management techniques and principles are essential for its success. The strict time constraints set for the project increase the difficulties of managing cost and quality. The project will be regarded as successful if the scope is finished on time, on budget, and to the required quality. Good quality means meeting the needs specified by the organizer, to the standard and specification laid down, with a predictable degree of reliability and uniformity, at a price consistent with the organizer's budget and to the satisfaction of the end users.

Learning Objectives

Through the study of this case, students should gain a better understanding of:
- The importance of project definition
- The relationship between the three project management dimensions; namely; time, cost, and quality
- The fact that a large and complex project, such as the Sydney 2000 Olympic Games, is a composition of a multitude of smaller sub-projects held in a fine balance and integrated into the overall project.

Discussion Questions and Possible Answers

1. Why is time management critical to the Sydney 2000 Olympics Games project?
    a. Time management is critical to the Sydney 2000 Olympic Games because on September 15, 2000, the eyes of the world will be focused on Sydney, and should the project not be completed, the world will judge it to be a failure. There will be a loss of face and credibility for the Australian government and enormous financial implications for organizers and commercial enterprises relying on the games to make profits. The definition of completed should not be limited to the completion of the infrastructure. The Sydney 2000 Olympic Games project will only be

complete when all the various systems, elements, sub-systems, and sub-elements have been trialed, tested, and proven in all their critical combinations and permutations. The instructor should encourage the student to discuss the hidden detailing that is required to make a project of this size and complexity a success. A project is not completed until it is fully commissioned. It may be difficult to estimate the time required to complete the commissioning phase, particularly in the planning phase, if the project definition is insufficiently detailed. The student could be asked how he might handle this with the discussion directed toward the importance of the study and appraisal of similar projects, such as the Atlanta 1996 Olympic Games, and using them as a base case on which to build. So even though every project is different, it still adds to the overall project management body of knowledge.

2. By what yardsticks will the Sydney 2000 Olympics Games project be measured, and how will it be considered a success? Give examples to illustrate your answer.

   a. The project will be regarded as successful if it is finished on time, on budget, and to the required quality. The instructor should encourage the student to illustrate her answer with examples of the various measurement criteria and interrelationship between these three conflicting demands. The student should be asked to review *PMBOK Guide*, section 1, What Is Project Management, and use this as a datum to answer this question.

3. Why is project scope management so important to the Sydney 2000 Olympic Games project? Illustrate your answer with some examples from projects that you have studied or worked on and draw parallels.

   a. The Sydney 2000 Olympic Games project is a very large and complex project. It is important that the scope be managed and controlled on all projects. With the Sydney 2000 Olympic Games project, it is critical to ensure the scope is managed for a number of reasons. Large public projects have a history of blowing out in both the time and cost dimensions. Good scope management will help to reduce the likelihood of this eventuating. It also will ensure that only the work required to successfully complete the project is included and that the overall project is not used as a shopping list by every self-interest group or as a mechanism to obtain unnecessary items that will affect the project's viability and success. Good scope management serves as a mechanism of scope change control (variations). Scope verification and acceptance will be essential to ensure the quality requirements are met and controlled. The instructor is referred to *PMBOK Guide*, section 5, Project Scope Management. The student should be encouraged to use examples from projects that he has studied or worked on and draw parallels.

4. A project is said to be successful if the work is finished on time, to cost, and to quality. We understand clearly how to measure time and cost-days and dollars-but few people have a clear idea of what they mean by quality in the context of projects. Discuss the concept of quality with specific reference to the Sydney 2000 Olympic Games project.

   a. For the Sydney 2000 Olympic Games project good quality means meeting the needs specified by the organizer, to the standard and specifica-

tion laid down, with a predictable degree of reliability and uniformity. There are three (3) essential elements to the concept of quality:
- Good quality versus high quality: Good quality does not imply high quality. The desired quality is defined by the purpose of the project. Various elements of the Games project will have different quality requirements.
- Fit for purpose: The concept of fit for purpose is often adopted as a measure of good quality and can be applied equally well whether the project is the Sydney 2000 Olympic Games security, opening ceremony, information system, or the transport system. If the project generates a product that is not fit for purpose, the product cannot be used or has little value to the customer and therefore is of poor quality.
- Conforming to the customer's requirement: Saying something is fit for purpose must come from the customer, and this implies that quality means meeting the customer's requirements or specification.

The instructor is referred to *PMBOK Guide*, section 8, Project Quality Management. The student is expected to illustrate how she would answer with specific examples that show that she understands the concept of quality.

ADDITIONAL DISCUSSION POINTS

The instructor may wish the students to conduct an audit of the Atlanta 1996 Olympic Games, or a component of them. Were the Atlanta 1996 Olympic Games considered a success or a failure? Why? Are there elements that the project managers of this project would have done differently if they could do it all over again? Has this knowledge been incorporated into the Sydney 2000 Olympic Games project?

Strategic Project Control Initiatives

Jose Herrero, Senior Project Director, Fluor Daniel
Dev Hundal, Principal Project Control Specialist, Fluor Daniel
Paul Russel, Senior Project Controls Engineer, Fluor Daniel

PMI Canada *Proceedings*, 1996, pp. 5–10

Synopsis

This case describes the implementation of a project controls philosophy to minimize the total installed cost of a petrochemical project in Alberta, Canada. This case also illustrates the use of the work process analysis and the obstacles of the transition from the design phase to the construction phase. The case discusses three strategic initiatives that allowed for major cost and schedule savings: early focus on planning, scheduling work packages, and the use of management tools to accelerate the transition from construction to completion.

Learning Objectives

The students will see how a project highly constrained by weather conditions and with a tight schedule was managed. From the questions and the class activity, the students will further understand the following key points:
- the phases of a project and their interdependence
- the relation between planning and the risks faced by a project
- the challenge and methods for handling a large amount of information
- the importance of risk management.

Discussion Questions and Possible Answers

1. The prime requirement of this project was clearly established. It was to minimize the total installed cost. The management of the project, in order to achieve this requirement and fulfill this project's objective, followed the strategy presented in Figure 1. Discuss the analogy between this strategy and the project management processes: initiating, planning, executing, controlling, and closing, listed in the *PMBOK Guide*, section 3.2, Process Groups.
    a. The strategy contains all of the five processes. They are just presented in a format which is easier for those involved with the project to understand. It could be difficult to identify a clear relationship between the elements in Figure 1 and the processes described in the *PMBOK Guide* because the figure is clearly customized for this project. However, the essence of the five processes is found in the diagram.

2. The case described a significant amount of planning as having gone into the project. How did this planning help to reduce costs?
    a. As is stated in the *PMBOK Guide* description of planning processes, section 3.3.2, the planning allowed risks to segments of the project and constraints affecting the project to be identified. Likewise, action was taken when planning tasks to account for these constraints and risks. For example, the early ordering of equipment to avoid delays and to allow work to be done by winter, as well as the identification of roadway restrictions on heavy equipment travel, were recognized and planned for. All of these travel plans were made well in advance of the project, planning which was beneficial for the project.
3. The risk and opportunity evaluation completed for this project identified several potential scheduling problems. How does this evaluation and its effect on scheduling affect cost management?
    a. Risk and opportunity evaluation recognized several potential scheduling problems, which would have led to significant delays in the project. These delays inevitably would have led to increased costs. By scheduling the project around such risks, costs can be better controlled allowing the fulfillment of the prime requirement, minimizing total installed cost, to be met.
4. The author stresses the importance of facilitating the transition between construction and completion (executing to closing the project). How did the project managers deal with this challenge?
    a. In order to close the gap between construction and completion, the project managers relied on the use of a control tool called the field progress reporting system (FPRS), when the key success factor was the ability to manage data from different databases related to manpower, progress forecasting, and work packages, therefore identifying the specific resources required for the completion of the activities.
5. Though the construction of this facility was a "cost-driven" project, cost management was not the only project management area used in the administration of the project. Mention at least two other project management areas involved in the making of this project.
    a. The knowledge areas of project management are each briefly described in section 1.3.2 of the *PMBOK Guide*. Each of these are key considerations in the successful administration of this and any other project.
6. This case describes how the natural environment affects all aspects of how the project work is done. Compare and contrast how these natural environmental risks are analogous to risks in other type of environments (i.e., public relations, political, etc.).
    a. There are similarities to all risks involved with projects, no matter their cause. Uncertainty must always be addressed and accounted for when planning a project. Some risks, such as the winter weather described in this project, can be scheduled for in order to minimize risk. Likewise, planning and care in the presentation of a politically risky project will help to minimize that project's risk.

ADDITIONAL DISCUSSION POINTS:

This case illustrates a project which is heavily dependent on weather and seasonal conditions. With the proper planning and control processes, it is possible to deal with these circumstances. The instructor may want to have the students identify similar uncontrollable factors and characteristics which need to be taken into account when planning a project.

    a. Suggestions: Natural phenomenon, government regulations and change, market changes, public attitudes, and behavior; all of these factors share the characteristic that they are not controllable by the project managers and the company in general but one can perform sensitivity analysis in order to determine the potential effects of these risks.

Libya: Redefining Challenge

Gordon Mahovsky, Project General Manager, RASCO Project

PMI Canada *Proceedings*, 1996, pp. 88–91

Synopsis

This case describes the $1 billion expansion of a petrochemical facility in Libya. The case presents the impact of international politics on project planning and execution due to the United Nations' sanctions on Libya and the civil war in former Yugoslavia. The direct effects on communication, travel, logistics, and human resource maintenance are discussed as well as other issues such as cultural differences. The paper does not go into the technical aspects of the plant but concentrates on the challenges and creative methods for dealing with unplanned obstacles in the running of the project.

Learning Objectives

After reading the case and answering the questions provided, the students will be able to:
- understand how to deal with uncontrollable factors
- understand the impact of international politics and the internationalization of the world economy
- realize the importance of human relations on projects
- gain a better understanding of the project manager's code of ethics.

Discussion Questions and Possible Answers

1. Due to political changes, the management of this project was faced with completely different challenges than it initially perceived. If, as a project manager, you are going to be involved with an endeavor with this characteristic, what management model would best suit your needs?

    a. To face new and non-controllable factors, the project should monitor these factors through use of a model such as that presented in Chapter 7, Strategic Issues in Project Management, of *Project Management: Strategic Design and Implementation*, 2nd ed., by Cleland. The output of this process can even include the generation of a new project. The process aims to deal with the effects of the non-controllable factors and the redefinition of the initial project phase. The management of project strategic issues can, according to Cleland, follow four phases: (1) identification of the strategic issues; (2) assessment of the strategic relevance; (3) analysis of the action required; and (4) implementation of the action selected to contribute to the resolution of the issue.

2. Human resources are discussed in this case, both from the staff/office and field staff/construction point of view. What are the difficulties and differences in managing these two different groups?

   a. The construction and field workers are able to see the project progress and gain satisfaction simply by witnessing this progression. Likewise, they have a rigorous but predefined work schedule (i.e., the Canadian group's seventy-two days in, twenty-one days out), which is clear. On the other hand, the office staff may see no other progress than the flow of paper through the office and staff jobs tend to be a regular weekly routine. The office staff may then need day-to-day incentives: recognition, luncheons, and other simple motivational techniques.

3. Can uncertainty such as the international political uncertainty described in this project be scheduled? When should the project management identify and evaluate such risks?

   a. It is very difficult to schedule for such risks. It is very difficult to foresee when such events as "international incidents" will cause problems for a project. However, these risks can be estimated during original project analysis and a determination can be made as to whether the project is worth the risk involved and what effects the incident will have on the project. Project risk management is discussed in *PMBOK Guide*, Chapter 11. Different techniques such as a decision tree, which considers the different possible outcomes and assigns probabilities and costs to these outcomes, can be used in the analysis of such risks.

4. The author mentions the procurement, transportation, communication, travel, and human resource problems faced in the course of the project. Among all of these problems listed, why did the job satisfaction and staff motivation become the priority of the project?

   a. Project management was really only able to address the problems of human resources. All of the other problems listed were outside of the scope and abilities of project management to address. For example, project management had no control over the airlines, telephone companies, or political climate.

   b. The morale of the project team is a key factor, especially when a project faces impediments and interference from non-controllable sources.

5. This case does not mention any problems in dealing with the Libyan government despite all of the international unrest surrounding Libya. How might the project management have successfully "sold" this project to the government?

   a. Economics. This project meant a great deal of money to Libya, both at the time of the project and in the future. Also, it allowed economic contact with non-United States First World countries. These motivations should have made it easy to explain to Libya, as a project stakeholder, the importance of the project.

6. The author ends the case with the phrase: "This project has demonstrated that, more than anything, people have made the difference and that the

most powerful tool in project management today still remains to be the human mind." Do you agree with this statement?

   a. With almost 100 percent certainty, yes. People are the core of all projects. People make all projects possible.

ADDITIONAL DISCUSSION POINTS:

The globalization of the world's economy and the restrictions on business in dealing with some countries such as the Libyan and Iranian United Nations' sanctions or the United States' embargo on Cuba have a great effect on project management. As a project manager dealing with these situations, how is one required to act? Should one attempt to work within the laws or find methods to get around the restrictions? Have the students research and discuss such regulations as the Helms-Burton Act, or other similar global sanctions, and the reactions of different stakeholders to them.

Discuss how PMI's Code of Ethics for the Project Management Profession relates to these questions (see Appendix A).

Land Reserve Modernization Project: The Future of Army Infrastructure

LCol. Foreman, Project Manager, Department of National Defense, Canada

PMI Canada *Proceedings*, 1996, pp. 101–7

Synopsis

This case describes the planning and building of a $100 million Militia Training Support Center at Meaford, Ontario, for the Canadian Armed Forces. The project faced some challenges due to cutbacks in budgets and the need to meet government regulations and policies. The case also describes other challenges the project faced including the bankruptcy of several contractors as they worked on the project. The project was completed one year ahead of schedule and 23 percent under budget. The case provides a clear look at the project management of a project which finished as a success despite several impediments to that success.

Learning Objectives

Through the study of this case, students should gain a better understanding of:
- project risk management
- project organizational structure
- the management of projects under multiple constraints
- project life-cycle costs.

Discussion Questions and Possible Answers

1. This project is described as unique, with a magnitude and scope not undertaken by the Canadian Army since the 1950s. How was this challenge taken?

    a. Because the tasks involved were out of the regular process of the Canadian Army, with a unique and new purpose, it was correctly considered a project. With the proper emphasis on planning and design, the project was implemented and completed with relative success.

2. Figure 1 of the case presents the project team organization. The author describes it as "a self accounting, independent, self contained organization that was dedicated to cradle-to-grave implementation of the project." Following the descriptions from section 2.3.3, Organization Structure, in the *PMBOK Guide*, what kind of organization was used for this project?

    a. The organization chart resembles a functional organization. However, the purpose of the whole organization is just this project. Therefore, each of the functions can be taken as subcomponents of the project and, thus, the chart would describe a project-oriented organization.

b. The structure could probably be described as a traditional hierarchical structure adjusted as necessary for the management of a project. The project brought about the use of teams and cross functioning units and essentially was a less structured organization than the traditional military framework.

3. This project had three contractors go bankrupt during the course of the project. These three contractors were responsible for almost one-third of the construction work on the project. However, all of the work involved with the project was completed on schedule and under budget. Given what was presented in the case and your own thoughts, how was this achieved?

    a. This successful completion was achieved in part through proper risk management. By developing solid contingency plans, such as the use of bonding companies to be responsible for the completion of work, the management of this project was able to assure timely and cost effective completion of this project.

4. It is clear from the case that the project took advantage of the economic situation of the area in order to "get the best value for the money from DCC's." However, this triggered the undesired side effects of the bankruptcy of several companies, substandard quality requiring remedial work, and delays in the schedule. This was the result of a component of project management not being carried out effectively.

    a. Project risk management was not able to cover all of the aspects of this project, allowing for these deficiencies. The management of the project disregarded the trigger effects of awarding the contracts based on reduced costs. Because the risks were not identified, actions could not be taken on time. Although the project was completed and called a success by the author, some quality problems did exist in the final product.

5. The project management officer was able to manage well enough to receive more responsibilities and gain control over a budget of $1 billion despite the fact that the Meaford camp was not a complete success. To what do you attribute this apparent disparity in additional responsibility and success?

    a. "Perfect is the enemy of good." The owners of a project will accept many underachievements in a project, such as inferior quality construction work. However, they will not tolerate the inability to achieve a project's intended deliverables. Because the Meaford camp was completed, albeit with some minor deficiencies, the project management officer was recognized as completing the project successfully.

ADDITIONAL DISCUSSION POINTS:

The life-cycle costs were described as requiring constant vigilance and value engineering. Is there ever a case when this is not necessary? Discuss.

Projects generally must be controlled on several levels, primarily from a scheduling and cost perspective. Project managers must be able to achieve the task of watching the schedule and financial bottom line while keeping a systems view of the project as well as knowing where the project intends to end. *PMBOK Guide*, section 3.3.4, Controlling Processes, describes the different processes required to maintain proper control.

R&D in the Insurance Industry: PM Makes the Difference

Julie M. Wilson, Implementation Manager, Pacific Mutual Life Insurance Company

PMI *Proceedings*, 1992, pp. 223–31

Synopsis

This case describes a reengineering process at Pacific Mutual Life Insurance Company (Pacific Mutual) and gives an excellent industry background. The project allowed the company to get the right products and services to the market on time with improved quality. The author stresses throughout the case the importance of blending people, processes, and technology. The case shows how Pacific Mutual is moving toward a more open and innovative culture, and how it has been successful in responding to the needs of its highly segmented market by the use of teams, organizational tools, and project management.

Learning Objectives

This case will allow the students to understand the wide applicability of project management. From the study of this case, students will further understand:
- the project life-cycle and the product life-cycle
- the importance of cross-functional teams and teamwork
- the importance of understanding the customer needs
- the barriers faced on the changing of a company's culture.

Discussion Questions and Possible Answers

1. In Figure 4, the author depicts the new project life-cycle. This life-cycle has six different phases, including an "implementation phase." Do you perceive this phase as having a clearly defined beginning and end, or do you think that this phase is occurring throughout the entire project?

    a. The case presents this phase as the culmination of previous phases, when all major tasks have been completed. Thus, implementation would start simultaneously at the beginning of the project. Peter W. G. Morris writes in *The Management of Projects*, in Chapter 8, The Management of Projects, The New Model, that there is a misconception that project implementation only starts after the project is defined and its relationships with external factors are identified. He states: "Implementation starts as soon as a project is conceived."

2. The general life-cycle for most products in the life and health insurance market is depicted in Figure 1. Do you see any resemblance between this life-cycle and a generic project life-cycle?

    a. In the *PMBOK Guide*, section 2.1.2, Characteristics of the Project Life-Cycle, the following characteristics are defined as common to most project life-cycles: "cost and staffing levels are low at the start, higher towards the end, and drop rapidly as the project draws to a conclusion." From this perspective, it can be said that the two life-cycles share some characteristics. However, the *PMBOK Guide* also warns of distinguishing between project life-cycles and product life-cycles. A project is undertaken to bring a product to the market and is but one phase or stage in the entire life-cycle of the product.

3. The case mentions that previously the term "on-time" meant differing things to different groups of workers. Therefore, groups completed tasks based on their own interpretation of what was necessary to complete that task. How is this problem addressed and solved through the new methodology?

    a. This problem is addressed through the use of cross-functional teams. This strategy allows team spirit to develop and to let members recognize the disadvantages of working as if they were in separate companies.

    b. The use of project management techniques also requires that schedule, cost, and technical performance objectives be established for each project.

4. The author states: "Because reengineering doesn't happen overnight, and because competitive conditions are increasing, now is the time for insurers to overhaul their business processes. Changes in the industry are accelerating and will continue to do so as less competitive companies are acquired by larger, more nimble companies." Do either of these statements (or both) apply to other industries with which you are familiar? Explain.

    a. Clearly the first sentence applies to many industries. Competition is increasing in manufacturing and service sectors. The second statement also applies to many industries. Allow the students to cite examples from their own experiences or from other literature.

5. The author mentions Pacific Mutual's core values of "openness, change, risk taking, accountability, and goal orientation." What barriers would the lack of these values present to a company trying to introduce project management teams?

    a. A lack of openness would inhibit teams since project teams must have the information and resources needed to make and implement decisions. Resistance to change inhibits any new process including the use of teams and project management. To effectively use a team approach, team members must be willing to take some risks and be held accountable for the decisions that are made. No team can function effectively without objectives, goals, and strategies.

    b. The instructor can further expand this discussion by letting students provide examples of other barriers to the team process. You may also wish to discuss how these barriers might be overcome.

ADDITIONAL DISCUSSION POINTS:

Thanks to the new methodology, Pacific Mutual was able to blend people, processes, and technology successfully. This methodology based its success on the use of cross-functional teams. The students should research and discuss the cultural characteristics prevalent in companies that are using teams.

Implementing Integrated Product Development: A Case Study of Bosma Machine and Tool Corporation

F. Paul Khuri, United States Air Force, Brooks AFB
Howard M. Plevyak, Jr., Air Force Institute of Technology, Wright-Patterson AFB

Project Management Journal, September 1994, pp. 10–15

Synopsis

This case studies the implementation of integrated product development (IPD) in Bosma Machine Tool Company (Bosma). The authors concentrate their analysis to the following six areas: changes to the work environment, team organization, training used, new team's group dynamics, rewards and incentives, and measures used to assess the success of the team. The case also offers useful inside information and recommendations on the management of newly formed teams.

Learning Objectives

Today's challenges required interdependent skills and approaches. This case will allow the students to further comprehend the following issues:
- the importance of teams
- the management of teams
- cultural barriers
- cultural changes due to teams.

Discussion Questions and Possible Answers

1. The Bosma Machine and Tool Corporation experienced a number of barriers during the transition to self-directed work teams from its previous organization. What were some of those barriers?

    a. The case identifies the following barriers:
    - accepting the responsibility of making decisions without management approval
    - team members were not certain of their empowerment
    - lack of communication within the team
    - fear of retaliation for voicing opinions
    - initial tendency of some team members to dominate early meetings
    - changing from a culture of following to one of leading
    - releasing traditional management controls

Organizing

- accepting self-management of the team
- no clear redefinition of the foreman's role.

2. When a new team is put together to run a project, anxiety among members can run very high. As a project manager said, "Moving a team member's desk from one side of the room to the other can sometimes be just about as traumatic as moving someone from Chicago to Manila." What can the project manager do in order to reduce the initial stress among team members?

    a. H. Kerzner, in *Project Management: A Systems Approach to Planning, Scheduling, and Controlling*, Chapter 5, Management Functions, suggests discussing the following with each team member:
    - what are the objectives of the project
    - who will be involved and why
    - the importance of the project to the overall organization or work unit
    - why the team member was selected and assigned to the project
    - what rewards might be forthcoming if the project is successfully completed
    - what problems and constraints are likely to be encountered
    - the rules of the road that will be followed in managing the project
    - what suggestion the team member has for achieving success
    - what challenge the project will present to individual members and the entire team
    - why the team concept is so important to project management success and how it should work.

    b. In addition to understanding the importance of working as a team to achieve the project's objectives, team members must understand "what's in it for me."

3. What are the characteristics of an effective team? Do you think these characteristics are present in less effective groups?

    a. O. Kharbanda and J. Pinto in *Successful Project Managers: Leading Your Team to Success*, Chapter 12, Team Building, state that the qualities that effective teams normally have are missing in less effective groups. The factors that most of the research lists as characteristics of successful teams include:
    - Clear sense of mission—The sense of mission must be collectively accepted by all team members and clearly understood.
    - Understanding the team's interdependencies—Team members have to know their contribution to the project and how their work fits into the overall endeavor.
    - Cohesiveness—How much attraction there is among team members and their tasks.
    - Trust—It is manifested in the belief among team members that they are able to disagree without concern about retaliation.
    - Enthusiasm—The belief among team members if the goal is achievable and the positive energy associated.

    b. Other characteristics of successful teams include: senior management support, interdisciplinary and diverse membership, integration into the organizational design, education and training, effective leadership, effective facilitation, clear team mission, objectives and goals, strong team chartering process, clear team roles and responsibilities, and a balance of authority, responsibility, and accountability (from Bursic, Karen M.,

Self-Managed Production (Manufacturing) Teams, in Cleland, David I., editor, *Field Guide to Project Management*.)

4. There are numerous examples in the literature of companies using self-directed work teams. Review the literature to find another example of the use of these kinds of teams. Discuss the organization of the teams and the benefits gained from their use.

    a. A good reference that discusses a number of examples of the use of these teams in industry is *Industry Week* magazine's annual profile of the winners of it's "best plants" awards. In one survey, *Industry Week* reported that all twenty-five winners and finalists in 1995 relied on empowerment practices and that 88 percent of those plants have launched self-directed work teams (production teams) to some extent (Sheridan, John H., Lessons From the Best, *Industry Week*, February 19, 1996, pp. 13–20.)

5. Some opponents of the team approach might argue that the culture of the United States is too individualistic to support this kind of organizational design and that Americans are not predisposed to work as part of a team. Defend or refute this position.

    a. A study conducted by a cultural anthropologist and marketing researcher in 1993 and 1994, and sponsored by the American Society for Quality Control, Disney, General Motors, Kellogg's, and Kodak, revealed three important findings that play a role in why teams fail. These include employees' need to know what's in it for them, people's previous unpleasant experiences with teams, and the individualistic nature of the American culture (Bemowski, Karen, What Makes American Teams Tick? *Quality Progress*, vol. 28, no. 1, January, 1995, pp. 39–43.) One of the major difficulties with teams in the United States is that the American culture goes against certain attributes called for in teams. In particular, many Americans have a strong need to have individual success at something. "Sacrificing" for the good of the team is not something Americans are predisposed to do. They also don't like to be "forced" to join a team. This resistance must be overcome if a team is to be successful. One of the ways to deal with this issue is to ensure that individuals as well as the team are recognized for contributions. This can be done by allowing each team member to play a particular role and make some type of contribution to problems that are solved and decisions that are made (Bursic, Karen M., Self-Managed Production (Manufacturing) Teams, in Cleland, David I., editor, *Field Guide to Project Management*).

ADDITIONAL DISCUSSION POINTS:

The case presents seventeen recommendations for implementing an integrated product team. The instructor might divide the class into small groups to discuss and present the consequences of not following these recommendations.

How ICL Used Project Management Techniques to Introduce a New Product Range

Peter Kayes, School of Technology and Information Studies, Thames Valley University, U.K.

International Journal of Project Management, October 1995, pp. 321–28

Synopsis

ICL was a product of the United Kingdom (U.K.) merger mania of the 1960s. Within a few years of its formation, ICL was in trouble. A new managing director was appointed from one of the major United States (U.S.) computer suppliers to the U.K. The case describes how project management techniques were used at ICL in the 1970s, and how they helped the company to cope with organizational challenges and to manage the risk of introducing a new product into the market. The author also speculates on the extent to which this project management approach has helped ICL through the 1990s, a period with major structural changes.

Learning Objectives

The transformation of this traditionally run company into a project-driven organization will help the students to realize the following issues:
- the characteristics of a functional organization
- the project manager role
- the customers importance
- project teams.

Discussion Questions and Possible Answers

1. This case illustrates how a traditional company was transformed into a project-driven organization. Describe the characteristics of a classic functional organization. What are some of the strengths and weaknesses of a functional organization?

    a. *PMBOK Guide*, Section 2.3.3, Organizational Structure, states: "The classical functional organization is a hierarchy where each employee has one clear superior. Staff are grouped by specialty, such as production, marketing, engineering, and accounting at the top level, with engineering further subdivided into mechanical and electrical."

    b. H. Kerzner in *Project Management: A Systems Approach to Planning, Scheduling, and Controlling*, Chapter 3, Organizational Structures, identifies the following advantages (table 3-1) and disadvantages (table 3-2) of the traditional organization, as paraphrased.

Advantages:
- Easier budgeting and cost control are possible.
- Better technical control is possible.
- It provides flexibility in the use of manpower.
- It provides a broad manpower base to work with.
- It provides continuity in the functional disciplines, policies, procedures, and lines of responsibility are easily defined and understandable.
- It readily admits mass production activities within established specifications.
- It provides good control over personnel, since each employee has one and only one person to report to.
- Communication channels are vertical and well established.
- Quick reaction capability exists, but may be dependent upon the priorities of the functional managers.

Disadvantages:
- No one individual is directly responsible for the total project (i.e., no formal authority, committee solutions).
- It does not provide the project-oriented emphasis necessary to accomplish the project tasks.
- Coordination becomes complex, and additional lead time is required for approval of decisions.
- Decisions normally favor the strongest functional groups.
- There is no customer focal point.
- Response to customer needs is slow.
- There is difficulty in pinpointing responsibility; this is the result of little or no direct project reporting, very little project- oriented planning, and no project authority.
- Motivation and innovation are decreased.
- Ideas tend to be functional oriented with little regard for ongoing projects.

2. Through the case, the author describes how the company, its products, and the relationships with its customers were transformed. What are some of the lessons of the cultural shift the company underwent during the 1970s?

   a. The author clearly states that the lessons from that period are:
   - the importance of focusing on customer needs
   - working toward the achievement of goals
   - proper allocation of resources
   - finding the reasons for things being done late or not being done, instead of giving excuses
   - empower managers to achieve their goals
   - support managers with the organization.

3. The author states: "In a highly technical area of development such as this, throwing resources at the problem does not necessarily solve it." Is this only true for technical areas?

   a. Certainly this statement is true for other areas of development as well. In any organizational transformation top management support is critical. However, this support must come not just from additional resources but from the appropriate resources and from providing project team members with the authority to make and execute decisions.

   b. The instructor may wish to augment this discussion by asking students to present situations from their own experiences when additional resources were unable to help or did not help solve a problem.

4. The author focuses on the importance of being "close to the customer." What is meant by this phrase and how is it accomplished?

   a. There is much discussion in the literature today about "designing for the customer" and producing products and services that not only meet but exceed customer expectations. It is critical that the project teams at ICL understand the technical requirements of the customer as well as other kinds of requirements (delivery schedules, after sales service, maintenance, etc.). By being "close to the customer" and deliberately involving customers in their project teams, ICL was able to accomplish this.

5. The author notes that an effective project manager must have a combination of technical and managerial skills. What other specific skills are critical for an effective project manager?

   a. The discussion about and answer to this question should include but may not be limited to the following: communication skills (listening and persuading), organizational skills (planning, goal-setting), team building skills (motivation, etc.), leadership skills (vision, leading by example, etc.), flexibility, creativity, patience, persistence, technological skills (experience with the technology as well as with project management tools and techniques), ability to delegate, ability to make and execute decisions, ability to manage conflict, and so forth.

ADDITIONAL DISCUSSION POINTS:

This case stresses the organizational transformation processes. The instructor might have students divide into two groups. One group should discuss and present a case for the use of a matrix organization while the other should discuss and present a case for the use of a functionally driven organization.

PMBOK Guide, Section 2.3.3, Organizational Structure, provides a general description of organizational design alternatives.

Motivating

3
MOTIVATING

Communication Strategies for Major Public Works Projects: The Los Angeles Metro Rail Program under Siege   73

Learning the Lessons of Apollo 13   75

Taxol®: An Example of "Fast-Track" Drug Development   77

Privatization in Patagonia: The Selling of Argentina's Largest Hydroelectric Plant   79

Quesnel Air Terminal: Design/Build Works in the Public Sector   81

The National Aero-Space Plane Program: A Revolutionary Concept   85

Communication Strategies for Major Public Works Projects: The Los Angeles Metro Rail Program under Siege

Rodney J. Dawson, Los Angeles County Metropolitan Transportation Authority

PMI *Proceedings*, 1995, pp. 56–61

Synopsis

This case describes the challenges that project managers faced in presenting the Los Angeles Metro Rail Program to the media and the public. Because the project had a great effect on the public through the traffic inconveniences which it caused, it was very much in the public eye. Project managers had to assure that a clear and accurate message concerning the status and benefits of the project were presented to the public. Through proper stakeholder management, the project managers would face fewer problems external to the project.

Learning Objectives

Through the discussion of this case, students should gain a better understanding of:
- the importance of stakeholder management
- the importance of communication management in a project which has a direct effect on the public
- the importance of keeping morale of workers high
- methods a project manager can use to deal with the media.

Discussion Questions and Possible Answers

1. This case describes both the media and political figures as possibly detrimental to this project. Describe the importance of properly communicating with the project stakeholders.
    a. Allow everyone to know what is happening in order to avoid surprises.
    b. Speak in a language the receptor is able to understand and by which they would not be threatened.
    c. The stakeholders will perceive less risk because they will have a better understanding of the project.
    d. Clear and truthful communications will improve the trust of the stakeholders.
    e. Accentuate the positives of the project and frame the negatives properly.

Motivating

2. Stakeholder management can be the key to the success of many projects. Develop a model which can be useful for any project for proper stakeholder management.

   a. The students can develop many kinds of models. The model should include the management cycle (motivating, organizing, planning, directing, and controlling) as related to stakeholder management. An example of a complete model is found in *Project Management: Strategic Design and Implementation*, 2nd ed., by Cleland, Chapter 6, Project Stakeholder Management. Figure 6.1 depicts the project stakeholder management process and describes seven steps in such process: (1) identify stakeholders; (2) gather information on stakeholders; (3) identify stakeholders' mission; (4) determine stakeholder strengths and weaknesses; (5) identify stakeholder strategy; (6) predict stakeholder behavior; and (7) implement stakeholder management strategy.

3. How would you handle the morale of workers and others on the project given the criticism aimed at the project?

   a. Make sure that the facts and truth about the project are clear and eliminate any uncertainty and gossip.
   b. Use the workers as spokespersons and as an example of the positive aspects of the project.
   c. Address the faults of the communication process causing the criticism.

4. The case suggests three conditions for success when communicating with the media. What are these? Can you think of any additional conditions?

   a. Present a simple story, personalize the story, and use symbolism to make the point.
   b. Avoid technical jargon which is hard to understand.
   c. Make sure the communication is well rehearsed and any questions are anticipated (cover your bases).
   d. Be very sensitive. Treat the media as the ears of the public and work to treat the media as the most sensitive listener in the public.

5. The author gives advice on handling communication with three different stakeholders. What are the common characteristics of the strategies?

   a. Talk about what the stakeholders are interested in.
   b. Promote trust through clear communication.

ADDITIONAL DISCUSSION POINTS:

The instructor may want to discuss the use of public relations as a key component in the project team. When is this required? When is it not needed?

Guidelines for communications management are provided in *PMBOK Guide*, Section 10, Project Communications Management. The four main sections of this chapter, Communications, Planning, Information Distribution, Performance Reporting, and Administrative Closure, describe the steps for proper communications management.

Learning the Lessons of Apollo 13

Michael S. Lines, PMP

PM Network, May 1996, pp. 25–27

Synopsis

This case develops a parallel between the Apollo 13 mission as depicted through the popular movie of 1995 and project management. Through the case, the author analyzes the key factors which allowed for the successful completion of the endeavor and how they apply to project management. These factors included: having a clear objective, picking the best people, and training constantly. Although the case does not go into great detail concerning the technical aspects of the Apollo 13 mission, it does cover many project management applications.

Learning Objectives

This case will provide the student with a general set of guidelines for a project. From the discussion of the case, the students will gain a better understanding of the importance of the following issues in the success of a project:
- the quality of the people involved in a project
- the characteristics of the team/project members
- the importance of the planning process
- the impact of a positive and proactive attitude
- risk management.

Discussion Questions and Possible Answers

1. List and discuss three parallels between the Apollo 13 mission and project management that the author points out.
    a. *Have a clear objective.* Without a clear objective, a project will lose focus from its original intention and its members will be discouraged.
    b. *Pick the best people.* Without the best or most appropriate people involved, a project may become mired on unimportant barriers.
    c. *Support them with the best team.* A good project team, not just the project manager, is necessary for achieving the objectives of the project.
    d. *Support them with the best equipment and technology.* Technology can be used to boost productivity of the project team.
    e. *Train constantly.* Training primarily beforehand as well as during a project assures a knowledgeable and well-prepared team through the design and implementation of a team development strategy.
2. Describe a project or even an everyday activity in which the unexpected happened. How did you handle it and did it work out? How does this ability to

deal with the unexpected play a part in project management? What are the major processes identified by the *PMBOK Guide* intended to deal with the unexpected?

  a. Risk management is an integral part of project management and must be considered in all projects. Project management teams are responsible for developing contingency plans throughout the life of a project. From the *PMBOK Guide*, section 11, Project Risk Management, the primary steps to follow when dealing with unplanned outcomes are: risk identification, risk quantification, risk response development, and risk response control.

3. If you have seen the movie, *Apollo 13*, you have become familiar with the personalities of some of the people who played a part in the mission. List some of their attributes which make them good members of a project team. Do you see any resemblance between these management skills and those identified by the *PMBOK Guide*?

  a. Leadership, persistence, flexibility, creativity, highly motivated, clear strength of vision, communicating, negotiating, problem solving, and influencing the organization. The *PMBOK Guide*, section 2.4, Key General Management Skills, presents five of the management skills listed above. All of the skills listed by the *PMBOK Guide* as well as persistence, creativity, flexibility, etc., above are important characteristics of project managers.

  b. The leadership style of other leaders could be used to emphasize effective and ineffective leadership styles.

4. The Apollo 13 project was an example of an effective team. What are the key characteristics of an effective team?

  a. From the book, *Strategic Management of Teams* by Cleland, Chapter 4, Team Development, the characteristics of an effective team are: (1) Members of the team feel that their needs for participating in meaningful activities in the enterprise have been satisfied through active membership on a team; (2) Team members contribute to the team's culture of shared work, interests, results, and rewards; (3) People on the team feel a strong sense of belonging to a worthwhile activity, take pride in the team activity, and enjoy it; (4) Team members are committed to the team, its activities, and achievement of its objectives and goals; (5) People trust each other, are loyal to the team's purposes, enjoy the controversy and disagreements that come out of the team's operations, and are comfortable with the interdependence of working on the team; (6) There is a large degree of interaction and synergy in the team's work; and (7) The team's culture is results oriented and expects high individual and team performance.

ADDITIONAL DISCUSSION POINTS:

Have the students discuss the influence of high pressure or stress on the success of any undertaking. Examples of stress can range from last-minute cramming for an exam to the work of a surgical team in an operating room. Have the students debate the positives and negatives of pressure on a project.

Taxol®: An Example of "Fast-Track" Drug Development

Gerald W. Crabtree, Bristol-Myers Squibb Company

PMI *Proceedings*, 1993, pp. 616–21

SYNOPSIS

This case describes a synergistic partnership between the drug manufacturer Bristol-Myers Squibb and the National Cancer Institute (NCI). The partnership's purpose was to develop a new cancer drug called Taxol® from the Pacific Yew tree (Taxus Brevifolia), to gain approval of the Food and Drug Administration (FDA), and to produce a sufficient amount of the drug in an extraordinarily short amount of time. This challenging project achieved its time goal remarkably well thanks to factors such as a close and good relationship with the project stakeholders (FDA and NCI) and cross-functional teams. The case describes the brief story of Taxol®'s initial development, its success, and its shortcomings.

LEARNING OBJECTIVES

From reading and discussing this case, the students will gain a further understanding of:
- the importance of having a clear goal in a project
- the responsibilities of the project manager
- the pros and cons of being a part of a successful team
- the synergy gained through a partnership
- the impact of clear and wide support from upper management.

DISCUSSION QUESTIONS AND POSSIBLE ANSWERS

1. What was the initial objective(s) of the project? What was the main reason for the achievement of this objective(s)?

a. The main goal was clearly to increase the supply of Taxol® so that the National Cancer Institute (NCI) could establish treatment referral centers to provide Taxol® therapy for appropriate patients until the new drug application was approved.

b. The reasons this was achieved were: the clear goal, the support of upper management and all of the company making this project the top priority, open line of communication due to the clear prioritization, and the profitable association between the NCI and Bristol-Myers Squib.

2. Bristol Myers and the NCI worked together to get Taxol® accepted quickly. How is this stakeholder relationship going to affect the long-term aspects of other related projects?

   a. This close relationship with NCI, essentially making it a stakeholder in the project, should enable Bristol-Myers to clearly communicate its tie with cancer patients. Long term, this relationship should allow the company access to the Food and Drug Administration (FDA) for other projects involving testing and development in the same area.

3. List a few characteristics of the described project manager's role which you would consider important.

   a. Arbitrator—Able to solve conflict using creativity.
   b. Liaison—Work with the FDA on the new drug application.
   c. Activities Coordinator—Assign and monitor the scheduled activities.
   d. Facilitator—Make sure that there are no impediments to project tasks. Additional information on the roles of the project manager are described in Chapter 16, Project Leadership, *Project Management: Strategic Design and Implementation*, 2nd ed., by Cleland.

4. After the new drug application had been passed, how would the project manager's job change?

   a. The project manager would no longer be a stress manager, but would remain as all of the other discussed roles. The project basically will begin a new life-cycle, given its new objectives, etc. The project life-cycle, as discussed in Chapter 11, Project Leadership, *Project Management: Strategic Design and Implementation*, 2nd ed., by Cleland, defines many of the roles of the project manager.

5. When working on the development of Taxol®, how should the project manager have managed and motivated project team members?

   a. It is described that the project manager tried to foster a "sense of pride" in the project from project team members. This was done through stressing the importance of the work as exemplified by the recognition of the Taxol® work as the priority in the company. The project manager should be conscious of the management of self as described by Cleland in *Project Management* (p. 346) and thus stress the importance and excitement of the work.

ADDITIONAL DISCUSSION POINTS:

This case comments on the issue of being part of the "star" project in the company. Some of the implications not covered in the case include such challenges as how to deal with former coworkers after joining a highly visible project. Have the students discuss the pros and cons of such status or success.

The discussion could begin with the responsibility for doing a good job and taking on new responsibilities, and dealing with possibly uncomfortable situations brought about by this success (envy of coworkers, power conflicts, etc.).

Privatization in Patagonia: The Selling of Argentina's Largest Hydroelectric Plant

H. Fred Smith, TransAlta Energy Corporation

PMI Canada *Proceedings*, 1994, pp. 34–40

Synopsis

This case describes the bidding and takeover of Argentina's Piedra del Aguila hydroelectric plant by a consortium of three utility companies from Canada, the United States, and Chile. The bid for the plant approached $1 billion. The case was told from the point of view of one of the representatives of the Canadian contingent. It describes the challenges of this type of international project and magnitude. The political environment and unrest in Argentina also presented challenges to the completion of this project. A project requiring the resources of multinational companies tests the capabilities of project management. The fact that this project ended a success is a testament to the power and capability of project management.

Learning Objectives

Through the study of this case, students should gain a better understanding of:
- the management of international projects
- project risk management
- the use of teams in project management
- the importance of language and cultural differences
- the day-to-day challenges in the management of a project.

Discussion Questions and Possible Answers

1. What was the primary objective of this project as described in the case?
    a. The primary objective seems to be to determine how to put together the bid offer for the hydroelectric plant. Developing this bid offer included determining if they should be in the bidding process at all, selecting the partners to bid with, and developing the bid.
2. According to the author, the bidding and takeover process described in this case "had all the classic elements of a project": a temporary undertaking, staff from different organizations, uncertain outcome, and dissolution upon project termination. Are there other elements to a project?
    a. In the *PMBOK Guide,* section 1.2, What Is A Project, a project is defined as "a temporary endeavor undertaken to create a unique product or service." Therefore, the definition given by the author is a complete description of a project based on the *PMBOK Guide.* It may be argued that

the definition does not consider goals, stakeholders, schedules, etc., but those are elements also shared with regular operations and not the key distinguished elements of a project.

3. List some of the risks to this project. How can they be handled?
   a. The Paleocauce (the ancient river channel which creates a geological problem).
   b. Taking over an existing project.
   c. Needing to move a population to the dam.
   d. The potential and existing political problems.
   All of these can be dealt with using the guidelines in *PMBOK Guide*, Chapter 11, Project Risk Management, which describes how to go about identifying, quantifying, and developing responses and contingency plans for the management of risks.

4. From the case, it can be inferred that at the beginning of the project, many of the actions in the project were not adequately planned. Most of the activities seemed to be reactive instead of proactive and uncertainty was a constant, as shown through the terrorist attack on the transmission towers. Is this common for all projects?
   a. The amount of planning in each project is not a constant. In this case, the initial activities were oriented to gather data and find out more about an interesting opportunity. There is not a rule as to how much planning each project requires. However, the planning stage is the best stage in a project to save future expenses.

5. Can uncertainty such as that caused by the multinational relationships described in this project be planned for? At what stage in the project can the project management identify and consider risks such as these?
   a. It is very difficult to schedule for such risks or barriers which might arise in the life of a project, such as the terrorist attack on the transmission towers or the different cultures among team members. Two areas of project management knowledge are required in order to adequately deal with these challenges. *PMBOK Guide*, Chapter 9, Project Human Resource Management, and Chapter 11, Project Risk Management, provide a framework for project managers to effectively deal with these circumstances.

ADDITIONAL DISCUSSION POINTS:

Throughout the case the author points out the synergy gained when the technical and financial representatives of the three companies started acting together instead of acting as six individual groups. Teams are becoming more and more important in business activities. Teams also have disadvantages. The students should research the disadvantages of teams and discuss.

A good source on the disadvantages of teams is Cleland's *Strategic Management of Teams*, Chapter 13, The Negative Side Of Teams.

Quesnel Air Terminal: Design/Build Works in the Public Sector

Tom W. Nash, Transport Canada, Airports Group
Ian Barrie, Public Works Canada, Air Transportation

PMI Canada *Proceedings*, 1994, pp. 105–9

Synopsis

This case describes the project of constructing a medium-sized (505 sq. m) air terminal in Quesnel, Canada. Having gone through deregulation in the 1980s, the air transportation industry in Canada faced many obstacles in the building of new terminals. This project presents the creative methods used to work within the government against the organizational inertia inherent in the government. Also, creative methods were used to address the concerns of the stakeholders involved in the project. This case also illustrates the design/delivery method which helped to cut costs and fulfill all of the regulatory requirements.

Learning Objectives

This public service project management case illustrates a new method of generating change without disrupting the organization. Through the analysis of this case, students will acquire a better understanding of:
- the variety of stakeholders in a project
- the importance and impact of interdisciplinary teams
- dealing with government agencies
- changing a system from within.

Discussion Questions and Possible Answers

1. This case illustrates how, due to the pressure from a group of stakeholders, the project found a creative way of achieving the desired result. Stakeholders are a very important element of any project. Develop a generic set of stakeholders for any project.

    a. From Cleland, *Project Management: Strategic Design and Implementation*, 2nd ed., p. 135, table 6.1, the regular stakeholders are: stockholders, creditors, employees, customers, suppliers, governments, unions, competitors, the local community, and the general public.

    b. From *PMBOK Guide*, section 2.2, Project Stakeholders, the key stakeholders on every project include: project managers, customers, performing organization, sponsors, owners, funders, suppliers, contractors, team members and their families, government agencies, media outlets, lobbying organizations, society, and individuals.

2. Who were the specific stakeholders for this project and what was their stake in the project?

   a. Transport Canada (designing and building of the terminal according to guidelines), the government agencies funding the project (investment and the fulfillment of building guidelines), the city and local who had chosen the Caribou theme (continuity of the city architecture and business for the community), the airlines (use of the terminal at a competitive rate), Public Works Canada (construction of the terminal), and the public (use of the terminal for travel).

3. This project worked with the public sector, and thus existed in the "fish bowl" of public scrutiny described. In order to continue funding for the project, the project management must be sensitive to its relationship with the public. How did project management deal with this concern successfully?

   a. The project management communicated and consulted with the public stakeholders, including them in the process, through this emphasis on communication and consultation and the use of steering committees, advisory committees, and technical committees. Also, these meetings were held with greater frequency and a larger range of expertise attending than those with non-public interests.

4. The use of the design/build method for the contractor allows the fulfillment of many goals and requirements of the stakeholders in an innovative manner. What are some of the advantages of this method that are mentioned in the case?

   a. Reduction of cost: Costs are reduced thanks to the early design changes implemented that required a low demand for rework. This method exploits the competitive advantages of the contractor at finding creative ways to fulfill the requirements of the job with flexibility.

   b. The involvement of the community: Through the involvement of the community and other prime stakeholders in the project, the contractor is assured the satisfaction of the stakeholders.

   c. With the acceleration of schedules less time will be spent between the design and building stages of the construction. Also, only one contractor will be involved in both stages of the construction.

5. The design/build method resembles an interdisciplinary team made up of members from engineering design and manufacturing. Due to the development of such a team, many positive effects are felt in the project. This type of team is also known as a product-process team or the concurrent engineering process. What are the advantages to this type of team or process?

   a. In *Project Management: Strategic Design and Implementation*, 2nd ed., by Cleland, on p. 64 there is a list of the advantages of this type of concurrent engineering effort. These include:

      1. Close interaction between engineering, marketing, and manufacturing.
      2. An increase in the possibility of success of the endeavor.
      3. Products/services get to the market sooner.
      4. Organizational resources are used more effectively and efficiently.
      5. People working in these teams have a higher degree of ownership of the product or process being developed.

6. Due to the different backgrounds and disciplines of the members of the team, the checks and balances encompass a wider range of considerations.

7. Time is saved. Time represents money and profits when the product or service is introduced into the market. Other information on this subject is included in *Strategic Management Of Teams* by Cleland, p. 198.

6. It is stated in the case that "listening to customers and addressing their concerns directly can have a revolutionary impact on an organization that traditionally defines project requirement for others." Compare this statement to the well-known Hawthorne effect, which shows that attention paid to employees impacts the conscientiousness of employees in their work.

   a. This "customer-driven" outlook of project management is quite similar to the attention paid to employees as shown through the Hawthorne effect. By expressing interest, the customer/employee reacts, and the relationship with that customer or employee is more active and perhaps even synergistic.

ADDITIONAL DISCUSSION POINTS:

Communities are becoming more and more aware of and involved with projects affecting their status and quality of life. Ask the students to form groups and have each of these groups identify a project of this type, involving a governmental agency, in their local community or country. The students should then identify the stakeholders of their project and list and discuss each stakeholder's stake in the project.

The National Aero-Space Plane Program: A Revolutionary Concept

Robert R. Barthelemy, Director, National Aero-Space Plane Joint Program Office
Capt. Helmut H. Reda, USAF, Plans Directorate, National Aero-Space Plane Joint Program Office

PMI *Proceedings*, 1992, pp. 490–93

Synopsis

This case describes the National Aero-Space Plane (NASP) program. The aerospace plane is an airplane capable of flying at twenty-five times the speed of sound. The authors discuss the project technical and environmental challenges and how these have been addressed. The case also illustrates the importance of innovative management in government mega-projects with competing contractors and thousands of personnel in hundreds of companies and universities.

Learning Objectives

After reading the case and answering the questions, the students will gain insight into the following issues:
- project objectives
- mega-projects management challenges
- selling the project to stakeholders
- management of government projects.

Discussion Questions and Possible Answers

1. The authors state: "Although the program must be focused on the goals of the NASP X-30 demonstrator, it must also generate the technology that will allow a broad basis for future hypersonic vehicles and derivatives of the NASP demonstrator." These two objectives are complementary but could potentially become conflicting. Discuss some of the key characteristics of the objectives of a project.
    a. According to H. Kerzner, *Project Management: A Systems Approach to Planning, Scheduling, and Controlling,* Chapter 7, Conflicts, project objectives must be:
    - "Specific, not general
    - Not overly complex
    - Measurable, tangible and verifiable
    - Realistic and attainable
    - Established within resources bounds
    - Consistent with resources available or anticipated
    - Consistent with organizational plans, policies, and procedures."

b. The instructor might also ask the students to discuss whether the NASP project objectives meet these characteristics. In particular, are the objectives "realistic and attainable" and "consistent with resources available or anticipated?"

2. By its characteristics, this project can be called a mega-project. This type of project requires special attention on certain issues. List some of the strategic issues you consider important for this kind of project. Do you think the managers of this project have addressed these issues? How would you define a mega-project?

   a. Cleland describes a strategic issue as "a condition or pressure, either internal or external, that will have a significant effect on one or more factors of the project, such as its financing, design, engineering, construction, and operation." This definition was derived from W.R. King and D.I. Cleland (eds.), *Strategic Planning and Management Handbook*. In Chapter 7 of D.I. Cleland's book, *Project Management: Strategic Design and Implementation*, he presents insight into how strategic issues in project management can be managed.

   b. A mega-project may be defined as one having the following characteristics: (1) extraordinary financing needs; (2) major political, economic, and environmental considerations during the design/engineering and construction phases and continuing upon project completion through operations; (3) experienced stakeholders ongoing involvement with potential liability if operational aspects are misjudged, misdesigned, or inefficiently operated; (4) major interdependent systems planning and control challenges; and (5) likely intense scrutiny by stakeholders such as medial and local communities.

   c. From O. Kharbanda and J. Pinto; *What Made Gertie Gallop: Learning from Project Failures*, Chapter 19, Megabucks to Megaprojects, following are critical activities for managing mega-projects:
   - Clearly articulate purpose and potential benefits.
   - Make conscious, up-front efforts to create and communicate a clear mission statement.
   - Develop and maintain a coalition of supporters (political and in the company).
   - Continuously monitor stakeholders.
   - Develop a positive attitude by owner, contractor, and the public in general.
   - Proper planning, clear schedules, and adequate backup.
   - Full attention to quality assurance and auditing.
   - Proper management of schedule.
   - Recognition of strategic issues.
   - Adequate financial analysis and clear budget limits.
   - Adequate project organization with effective leadership, resources, and communications management.
   - Acceptance that the project is made up of people and they are not perfect.
   - Teamwork and culture.

3. Discuss some of the project benefits that can be highlighted when communicating with the general public about this project.

   a. Besides the aero-space technological advance, the project manager can point out the importance of developing new materials and their potential applications in everyday life, the increased understanding of the environment of the project, and any other type of benefits that the general public can understand and accept.

4. There have been cases of mega-projects (such as the superconducting supercollider project) that have been terminated after several years of work. Discuss the importance of knowing when to terminate an unsuccessful project. Is there a possibility that the NASP project might have the same fate?

   a. Because project team members often take personal pride in a project and feel a sense of ownership, termination is often difficult. There are a number of questions that should be considered to gain insight into whether a project should be terminated, including:
      - Does the project continue to fit in the strategic plans of the organization (the United States, in this case)?
      - Does the project complement strengths of the organization and avoid dependence on weaknesses in the organization?
      - Will the project achieve its goals?
      - Will completion of the project help the organization achieve its mission, objectives, and goals?
      - Can the owner continue to assume the financial and other risks associated with the project?
      - Will the project help the organization become more competitive? (Adapted from Cleland, 1994, *Project Management: Strategic Design and Implementation*, Chapter 14, Project Termination)
   b. Unless the project managers clearly outline the benefits of the project to the United States citizenry and gain public acceptance of those benefits, it could easily have the same fate as the superconducting supercollider. The project mission and objectives do seem to be clearly specified in this case.

5. Identify the stakeholders in this case and discuss their role in the project.

   a. The stakeholders of this project include the United States government, the general public, the five major airframe companies, the three leading engine companies listed in the case, the Air Force, Navy, SDIO, NASA, and DARPA, as well as several universities and researchers at those universities. All of these stakeholders have particular interests in the project. From the general public perspective, the concern is over whether tax dollars are being spent prudently. From the industrial companies viewpoint, the focus is on the profitability of their part of the project. The United States government and its agencies must be concerned with the strategic advantages of completing the project.

ADDITIONAL DISCUSSION POINTS:

This project has the potential to change the air transportation business as it is known today. The international characteristics of the world economy and the dissolution of the Soviet Union have removed many of the financial and technological boundaries among countries. The students can discuss the role of mega-projects in today's world, as well as research the current status of the NASP X-30.

DIRECTING

4 DIRECTING

Quality Management Works 93

Destroying the Old Hierarchies 95

Saturn's Vision for Program Management: A Different Kind of Approach 99

Using Project Management to Create an Entrepreneurial Environment in Czechoslovakia 101

The Channel Tunnel: Larger than Life, and Late 103

Minimizing Construction Claims under the Project Management Concept 107

Quality Management Works

Tony Yep, Project Manager, Bantrel Inc.

PMI Canada *Proceedings*, 1996, pp. 40–45

Synopsis

This case describes the benefits and uses of quality theories in management as applied in the ARCO corporation. The author is a project manager who espouses the use of quality endeavors including: teamwork, empowerment of employees, clear and constant communications, and employee recognition systems. The author concludes that the use of these quality initiatives has both tangible and intangible benefits for ARCO. He also concludes that the use of these initiatives allows for a more effective project manager.

Learning Objectives

Through the study of this case, students should gain a better understanding of:
- the implementation of quality initiatives
- the benefits of quality management
- project communications management
- the effective use of status review meetings.

Discussion Questions and Possible Answers

1. In order to facilitate communications on the project, team members with different responsibilities were seated next to each other. How would this affect diverse team members, such as those in production and design?
   a. This arrangement should have a favorable effect on the project as a whole because it encourages communication. Communications should make the design team more empathetic to the production team's needs. This arrangement will not only expedite communications but will also allow for more effective and clear communications between the teams.

2. This project used a creative method for dealing with status review meetings. Why was it possible and useful to use this type of control system?
   a. The status review meetings, brief meetings which initially were held daily, allowed for communications between all segments and from all levels of the project team. The emphasis on empowerment and trust within the company brought about by this total quality orientation of the company allowed for this. These meetings served as formal and informal sessions allowing full team participation.

3. The author of the case made reference to several total quality theories of Deming, Juran, and Crosby. Which of these points do you consider most important to the success of the project? Discuss.

   a. The references address the topics of people and trust, team concepts, team buy-in and empowerment, effective communications, recognition, management style, and the benefits of total quality management. All of these topics are important because all of these concepts are required for the success in any endeavor embracing total quality management.

4. What are the benefits of the recognition programs, free luncheons, and teamwork training sessions? As a project manager, is it your responsibility to coordinate efforts such as these?

   a. These efforts all serve to motivate project team members, build teamwork skills, and improve the morale of the project team members. The culture of the corporation will determine to what extent efforts such as these are the responsibility of the project manager. However, as a project manager, it is expected also that one acts as a leader, and thus takes on the responsibility of addressing these issues. By showing the support of top management with these issues, the employees will be more inclined to work toward the quality aspects as well.

5. Do the concepts presented in this case match all that you have read, heard, and learned concerning project management? Given what you have read in this case, is a project manager also a total quality manager?

   a. Most of the concepts concerning total quality management are in some way addressed in the work on project management. Total quality management's focus on the human aspect of work is not quite addressed in the *PMBOK Guide*. This is because it is beyond the scope of the *PMBOK Guide*, due to its involvement in a completely independent body of knowledge. However, effective project management addresses the concerns and theories of human resources management and motivational theory.

ADDITIONAL DISCUSSION POINTS:

Discuss the lists describing traditional and quality management techniques. Are these methods reconcilable? Is there ever a time when traditional management techniques are preferred?

The last quotation in the case is: "If you always do what you've always done, you'll always get what you have always gotten ..." The instructor may want the students to research the topic of paradigms and change, and discuss their findings.

Destroying the Old Hierarchies

Seth Lubove

Forbes, June 3, 1996, pp. 62–70

Synopsis

This case describes the organizational transformation of Boeing fostered and directed by new CEO Philip Condit. The creation of hundreds of integrated "design-build" teams, inspired by the success of the 777 project, has changed the way in which things are done at Boeing. The result is a more flexible and efficient company supported by teams. This case illustrates the importance of interdisciplinary teams and the close relationship between Boeing and its projects.

Learning Objectives

This case will allow the students to understand the growing importance and impact of teams. From reading the case and answering the questions provided, the class should:
- understand the pros and cons of teams
- understand the current organizational trend at Boeing
- realize the importance of cost management in low margin industries
- learn about the importance of interpersonal skills in leadership.

Discussion Questions and Possible Answers

1. The article mentions that former CEO Frank Shrontz considered interpersonal skills as one of the most important characteristics of his successor. What are some of the key management skills needed to run a project or enterprise? Support your answers with information from the *PMBOK Guide*.

   a. Section 2.4, Key General Management Skills, of the *PMBOK Guide* lists the following as key management skills: leading, communicating, negotiating, problem solving, and influencing the organization. All of these skills are necessary for a leader to effectively manage his project. Extended definitions of each of these skills are provided in the *PMBOK Guide*.

2. The labor union/management relationship at Boeing had been very antagonistic in the past and remains tense. How is Boeing's new CEO Philip Condit attempting to ameliorate these relations?

   a. Condit is attempting to improve the relations with the unions which work with Boeing through several methods. Some of the methods used are: compromise (not firing workers when outsourcing), recognizing the importance of the workers (design-production teams), sending everyone in the company an annual report, and through personal communications with employees (talking with picketers and workers).

3. The biggest change made by Condit on the 777 project from previous Boeing endeavors was the organizational design. "Working together" challenged all the former ways of doing things and brought together the design and production areas of Boeing. The undertaking of this endeavor was supported by teams. Does this management approach have any resemblance to the work organization utilized in project management?

   a. Teams are inherent to projects. Through projects, companies try to bring to life the future of an enterprise. The process of dealing with change always requires the involvement of diverse areas such as design, marketing, production, finance, and sales in order to run the project.

4. Boeing is one of the three major players in the airline production industry, with AirBus and McDonnell Douglass as the other two major companies. How does this small amount of competition affect the selection and management of projects?

   a. Costs and profitability are very important in the selection and management of projects. Because of the easily recognizable competition, there are clear monetary limits and necessities associated with projects. This makes project cost management key when managing a project. Chapter 7 in *PMBOK Guide*, Project Cost Management, discusses methods for the effective management of this aspect of a project.

5. Why is the use of interdisciplinary teams for product design, also known as concurrent engineering, a key element of projects and of regular management activities?

   a. In order to create or redesign a product or service, or in the everyday activities of a company, the synergy generated through the use of teams creates the energy that allows companies to deal with daily and future challenges.

   b. Teams are in many ways a miniature representation of an entire organization. They are often made up of members from different areas of the organization. Because of their size, teams are flexible and have a free flow of information among the members allowing them to deal with ad hoc problems and opportunities.

6. How does the title of this case, "Destroying The Old Hierarchies," describe what is going on at Boeing?

   a. Hierarchies are being broken in that changes are being made in the management and operations of the company. These changes include such things as the reduction of layers of authority and changes in the responsibility and accountability relationships. Communications with the workers are being improved and profitability is being focused upon. Much of this is being done through the management of the 777 project which is driving change necessary for the future of Boeing.

ADDITIONAL DISCUSSION POINTS:

The *PMBOK Guide*, section 2.3, Organizational Influences, presents and discusses different kinds of organizational charts. With the increasing importance of teams in the organization, do you think that a new type of chart should be developed and included in the future? Discuss.

A good description of that new structure (teamocracy) can be found in Cleland's *The Strategic Management of Teams*, Chapter 2. Teamocracy is the use of teams in organizations for bringing about cross-functional and cross-organizational work. The teams serves as a social unit based on empowerment and leads to the acceptance of an organization member's responsibility and accountability.

Saturn's Vision for Program Management: A Different Kind of Approach

Lisa W. Churitch, Saturn Corporation
Denis P. Couture, Integrated Management Systems, Inc.
Clement L. Valot, Integrated Management Systems, Inc.

PMI *Proceedings*, 1992, pp. 74–80

Synopsis

This case describes Saturn's organizational structure based on functional, cross-functional, and development teams. The author illustrates how work breakdown structures are used to accommodate planning and management requirements by functional systems (function) and by vehicle systems (project). The case offers a view of the development and management of schedules and how these are develop by each center of interest.

Learning Objectives

This case will allow the students to realize the growing importance of teams. From reading the case and answering the questions provided, the class should:
- understand the matrix organization, its advantages and disadvantages
- the wide application of project management concepts
- gather better understanding of the Saturn corporation
- the importance and management of schedules.

Discussion Questions and Possible Answers

1. The case mentions some of the shortcomings of a matrix organization structure including troubles in developing plans and resolving problems when "local" and program-wide objectives are in conflict. Define the meaning of a matrix organization structure and list its disadvantages.

    a. The matrix organization structure is a middle point between a pure product/project and a pure functional organizational structure. Personnel from functional departments will have functional and product/project responsibilities as well as functional and project superiors. Disadvantages, described by *Project Management: A Systems Approach to Planning, Scheduling, and Controlling* by Harold Kerzner, in Chapter 3, Organizational Structures, include: multidimensional information and work flow, dual reporting, changing priorities, opposing management and project goals, potential for conflict, difficult monitoring and controlling, biased functional managers, and difficult managing of functional project/organization balance of power and role ambiguity.

2. This case defines Saturn's program management, but seems to focus on scheduling. How are Saturn's cross-functional teams used in the development of schedules?
   a. The expertise and flexibility of the cross-functional teams are used to integrate schedules, such as to bring parts of the car development process together. Schedules are owned by teams, they are responsible for their development and update, and for their accuracy and completeness.
3. The matrix organization structure emerged in the early 1960s as an alternative to the functional structure. This organizational form enjoyed popularity in the 1970s and early 1980s. What are its main advantages?
   a. Advantages to the matrix organizational structure, described by *Project Management: A Systems Approach to Planning, Scheduling, and Controlling* by Harold Kerzner, in Chapter 3, Organizational Structures, include: distributed stress; shared authority and responsibility; specialist and generalist capabilities generated; time, cost, and performance are better balanced; minimized conflict; functional organization supports the project; rapid response to change, conflicts, and project needs; project manager has authority to commit resources; separate policies and procedures can be established for the project; project manager has complete control over all resources; program cost is minimized; and project team members have a "home" to return to after the project is terminated.
4. The description of program management teams in the case describes teams being led by marketing during the development phase and engineering and manufacturing during the implementation phase. How might this varying leadership affect the performance of the teams?
   a. It may slow the team's progress during the transition due to new leadership, but the change in focus should be beneficial when working on the distinctly different phases of the project. The leadership of the project, however, should not matter if the teams are properly developed and empowered.
5. The process required to develop a Saturn vehicle is organized through the use of two work breakdown structures. Describe those two breakdown structures. What kind of organizational structure does their creation resemble?
   a. The two breakdown structures defined are:
   Vehicle System Breakdown: The product is organized into areas with content crossing multiple functional teams (i.e., door).
   Functional System Breakdown: The product is organized into its functional content crossing multiple vehicle systems (i.e., electric).
   There is not a resemblance to a specific organizational structure. It could be stated, however, that the structure resembles a matrix design. Yet, Figure 4 in the case depicts components definition, clearly referring to work and not to people. Thus, a work package is defined, not an organizational structure.

Using Project Management to Create an Entrepreneurial Environment in Czechoslovakia

John Tuman, Jr., Institute for Management Technologies, Inc.
Moses Thompson, Team Technologies, Inc.

PMI Proceedings, 1992, pp. 405-9

Synopsis

This case describes the authors' consulting experience with Czech and Slovak managers on their managerial transformation process toward a free market economy. The case illustrates the problems faced by the organizations and their executives, and the potential of the project management discipline on entrepreneurial ventures, environmental projects, joint ventures, and privatization programs. The authors stress the importance of effective leadership, adequate and proper planning, cultural differences, project design, and team development.

Learning Objectives

The development of this case will expose the students to valuable insight into the project management discipline, such as:
- the differences between a manager and a leader
- the role of planning and its importance
- the wide applicability of project management
- cultural differences.

Discussion Questions and Possible Answers

1. The authors state that they found Czech and Slovak managers familiar with traditional scheduling technology, but without project manager expertise. Therefore, they aimed their training programs toward the planning function and its relationship with project implementation and evaluation. Discuss the importance of project planning.

    a. According to H. Kerzner, *Project Management: A Systems Approach to Planning, Scheduling, and Controlling*, Chapter 11, Planning, the four basic reasons for project planning are:
    - "To eliminate or reduce uncertainty
    - To improve efficiency of the operation
    - To obtain a better understanding of the objectives
    - To provide a basis for monitoring and controlling work."

2. The case describes several weaknesses found on project designs such as: lacked clear statement of purpose or impact, lacked clear performance measures, etc. The authors state: "These weaknesses needed to be addressed during the project design phase where the cost of planning is significantly less than during implementation." Do you agree with this statement? Why?

   a. Yes. The *PMBOK Guide,* Section 2.1.2, Characteristics of the Project Life Cycle: "The ability of the stakeholders to influence the final characteristics of the project product and the final cost of the project is highest at the start and gets progressively lower as the project continues. A major contributor to this phenomenon is that the cost of changes and error correction generally increases as the project continues.

3. The Czech and Slovak managers were anxious to learn about being a leader, what it is the difference between a manager and a leader?

   a. Managers do things right. Managers plan, organize, motivate, direct, and control particular activities. Leaders do the right thing. Leaders carry out a vision. Although managers are required to lead, leaders may not always be managers.

   b. The *PMBOK Guide,* Section 2.4.1, Leading, states that managers are concerned with producing results expected by stakeholders. Leaders are the ones who give direction to the organization (vision), align people (build consensus around the ones needed to achieve the vision), and motivate and inspire people in order to energize them into overcoming the obstacles and barriers to change.

4. Discuss the importance of recognizing cultural differences when implementing project management and list examples of cultural features relevant to this case.

   a. Culture is a set of refined behaviors that people have and strive toward in their society. A society's culture will naturally have significant effects on an organization's culture. An organization's culture consists of shared explicit and implicit agreements among organizational members as to what is important in behavior, as well as attitudes expressed in values, beliefs, standards, and social and management practices (Cleland, *Project Management: Strategic Design and Implementation,* 2nd ed.). Thus, the organizational culture will have effects on project management.

   b. In this case several cultural features were noted including: lack of individual initiative (brought about by forty years of centralized government planning), little experience working in teams, and little interest in customer satisfaction.

ADDITIONAL DISCUSSION POINTS:

The instructor might ask each student to consider a country other than the United States with which she is familiar and discuss the cultural features of that country that might inhibit or promote the use of project management techniques.

The Channel Tunnel: Larger than Life, and Late

Virginia Fairweather

Civil Engineering, May 1994, pp. 42–46

Synopsis

The Channel Tunnel linking Great Britain and France is an engineering achievement and symbol of man's imagination and daring. But it is also the one of the world's largest private financial failures. The author describes this mega-project from the perspective of five executives involved in the endeavor. The case presents the potential reason for the financial shortcomings of the project and offers insight into the organizational challenges.

Learning Objectives

From this unsuccessful project and the discussion of the case, the students will acquire a better comprehension of:
- conflicts with stakeholders
- project scope management
- financing a project
- the importance of the balance between planning and implementing.

Discussion Questions and Possible Answers

1. Despite facing many management failures, the Channel Tunnel is certainly one of the world's engineering wonders. The author concentrates her analysis on the conflict between Transmanche Link (TML) and Eurotunnel. Suggest a course of action that should have been taken to prevent this conflict.

    a. Among other reasons, the conflict arose due to the misunderstanding of the lump-sum contract by Eurotunnel and TML. Some ways to avoid this problem include allocating enough time for the planning stage of the project and the use of proper project scope, cost, and procurement management.

2. Some of The Intergovernmental Commission (ICG) decisions caused a portion of the cost overrun on the project. As a project manager, what could you have done to minimize the impact of these decisions?

a. *PMBOK Guide,* Section 11, Project Risk Management, has four processes—risk identification, quantification, response development, and response control—that give some insight into how to handle this kind of situation. These processes are defined as follows:
- "Risk Identification—determining which risks are likely to affect the project and documenting the characteristics of each.
- Risk Quantification—evaluating risk and risk iterations to assess the range of possible project outcomes.
- Risk Response Development—defining enhancement steps for opportunities and responses of threats.
- Risk Response Control—responding to changes in risk over the course of the project."

b. Certainly, not all risks can be anticipated but an effective risk management process can help to alleviate the effects of many unplanned events.

3. In an interview in the article, one executive, in referring to the bank and contractor who put the project together, said that they "had no idea how to be owners." What is the role of the owner of the project? Where did the owners of this project fail?

   a. Peter W. G. Morris in *The Management of Projects,* Chapter 8, The Management of Projects, The New Model, states that owners generally have three roles:
   - "To ensure that the project as conceived and realized meets its objectives." (Sponsor's role) This is the most critical one.
   - "The task of ensuring that once handed over operations, the product will perform optimally." (Operator's role).
   - "Ensuring that the project is realized effectively and efficiently." (Builder's role).

   b. In addition, the owner must provide funds for the work and may provide any required insurance and indemnity, approve changes, obtain permits, resolve conflicts, and establish standards.

   c. The article points out that the biggest mistake of the project owners was allowing the lump-sum contract for the fixed equipment. This contract was inappropriate for a project of this nature that had never been done before. Apparently, the owners were pressured into agreeing to it.

4. List some of the other factors that might have contributed to the cost overruns and schedule delays on this project.

   a. Answers to these questions might include such issues as the lack of understanding of the technical aspects of the project by the owners, political impacts that were not anticipated, late changes to the design for safety and security, varying contracting and payment methods, the involvement of multiple governmental agencies, etc.

ADDITIONAL DISCUSSION POINTS:

This project had to face many challenges and certainly more has been written about this mega-project. The instructor might ask the students to research other reasons for the managerial failure of this project. Two viewpoints from the literature are worth noting:

- Peter W. G. Morris in *The Management of Projects*, Chapter 7, The 1980's: Expansion of the Strategic Perspective of Managing Projects, states that the problem was "the old problem of concurrency—of starting construction before the design is properly worked out."
- O.P. Kharabanda and J.K. Pinto in, *What Made Gertie Gallop: Learning from Project Failures*, Chapter 15, The Channel Tunnel: Is There Light at the End?, suggest among other problems that the old love/hate relationship between France and England may have had an important influence on the project.

Minimizing Construction Claims under the Project Management Concept

Regula A. Brunies, Revay and Associates Limited
Ross Brophy, Public Works and Services, Government of Newfoundland and Labrador St. John's

PMI Canada *Proceedings*, 1986, pp. 198–212

Synopsis

This case presents some of the techniques used by a project owner to successfully complete a $42 million construction project within budget, on time, and without claims. This particular project involved the construction of a major educational facility in St. John's, Newfoundland. Specifically, the case discusses the use of an independent, third-party consultant to perform some of the traditional project manager's functions in an attempt to reduce some of the project risk. The case also describes some "risky" project management practices being used in the construction industry. Finally, the case presents some of the problems and concerns that, for the most part, are unique to the island of Newfoundland.

Learning Objectives

This case provides the students with an overview of some of the risks and concerns associated with a construction project. In particular, the student will be exposed to some unusual problems and risks that are unique to the particular construction project described in the case. As a result, the student will indirectly see the need to consider the project's environment and all of the potential risks. The following points should be addressed when discussing the case:
- the importance of considering all project risks, especially those that are unique to the particular project
- how using poor project management practices may also lead to risk
- how adding a third, independent party to a contractor-owner relationship can be used to reduce project risk.
- how to reduce risks through the effective design and testing of a project monitoring and control system.

Discussion Questions and Possible Answers

1. What are some of the key management skills needed to run a project or enterprise? Support your answers with information from the *PMBOK Guide*.
    a. Section 2.4, Key General Management Skills, of the *PMBOK Guide* lists the following as key management skills: leading, communicating,

negotiating, problem solving, and influencing the organization. All of these skills are necessary for a leader to effectively manage his project. Extended definitions of each of these skills are provided in the *PMBOK Guide*.

2. What problems were encountered under the project management concept in this case?

   a. In the past, the Department of Public Works and Services had chosen to use the project management method on the larger, more complex construction projects. Later, however, its use of this approach resulted in lengthy delays, high cost overruns, and a large number of claims. The student should also point out that, although these problems were encountered while using project management techniques, they may actually have occurred from how the techniques were applied rather than from the project management system itself.

3. Describe the "risky" practice that was leading to some of these problems, including some of the overriding factors that negated any projected benefits.

   a. The primary cause of these project problems appears to be the practice of "fast-tracking," in which the work packages are rushed to the field, with the design being completed after construction has begun. Although the concept of "fast-tracking" may initially appear to provide substantial benefits with only a minimum amount of risk, the case identified the following risks associated with "fast-tracking":
   - The planned benefits to be gained were usually lost due to schedule delays.
   - The additional financial benefits offered were also lost due to the cost of claims and litigation.
   - The contractors were intentionally submitting low bids and unrealistic schedules because of incomplete specifications. In essence, the contractors planned to regain their money by overpricing any extra work required on the subsequent change orders.

   Obviously, any errors made in the early design/engineering would have far-reaching effects on the overall project.

   By rushing these work packages out to the field, it would be difficult to develop a firm schedule or cost estimate. Since the schedule and cost of these work packages would be in a state of constant revision, it would be virtually impossible to have a reliable project management system. Finally, a study concluded that the risks associated with the practice of "fast-tracking were far too great and unpredictable."

4. Describe the modified project management approach used to reduce some of these risks.

   a. First, the company decided to use the "phased-construction" approach as opposed to the more risky "fast-tracking" approach. In the "phased-construction" approach, the design of a work package is nearly complete when construction begins. In addition, the traditional project management approach was modified with the introduction of an independent auditing/quantity surveying consultant. This consultant would be responsible for the preparation of detailed contractor-type construction estimates, master scheduling, and for monitoring of project costs and schedule progress.

5. What risks was the Department of Public Works and Services trying to reduce by adding another consultant to the project management team?

   a. Based on their experience, project/construction managers tend to over or underestimate the proposed budget and/or schedule for a project. By introducing a third, independent party these tendencies might be effectively minimized. This independent party can perform the same tasks traditionally carried out by the project/construction manager, such as scheduling, estimating, and monitoring, without any conflict of interest. Recent court decisions have made it more beneficial to have projects monitored by an unbiased party who has no financial interest and can respond quickly. In short, the court holds the project owner responsible for paying a contractor's claim that resulted from neglect or delay on the owner's part. The use of a third, independent party is also a preventive type of measure that is less costly then any lengthy court battle. Finally, this neutral third party can also serve as a mediator to resolve disputes and potential claims between the owner and contractors.

6. What were some of the contributions made by the auditing/quantity surveying consultant? How did these contributions minimize project risk?

   a. Based on a preliminary analysis, and considering the risk of a possible construction strike, the consultant concluded that the project could be completed about ten months earlier than planned. It was the owner who had advised the project manager to overestimate the schedule so as to eliminate the risk of not completing the project on time. In short, the project manager was much too cautious on his "no risk" schedule projections. As a result, a revised schedule was later agreed upon by all the involved parties. In order to minimize the confusion and potential for claims, the consultant warned against incorporating vague dates in the tender documents in lieu of an approved project schedule. Rather than trying to base a cost estimate on incomplete drawings and conflicting documents, the consultant decided to work hard to complete the documentation upon which these estimates were based. As a result of these efforts, the consultant effectively reduced the risk of erroneous cost estimates. While preparing the construction cost estimate, drawings were being continuously revised and corresponding adjustments were being incorporated into the cost estimate. The consultant's estimating team also realized the need to rely on one of its members who was familiar with the area of Newfoundland.

7. What actions can be taken by project managers to minimize some of the associated risks before starting to monitor a project?

   a. *PMBOK Guide*, Section 11, Project Risk Management, suggests four steps in managing risk: risk identification, quantification, response development and response control, which gives some insight into how to handle this kind of situation. These processes are defined as follows:
      - Risk Identification—determining which risks are likely to affect the project and documenting the characteristics of each.
      - Risk Quantification—evaluating risk and risk iterations to assess the range of possible project outcomes.
      - Risk Response Development—defining enhancement steps for opportunities and responses of threats.

- Risk Response Control—responding to changes in risk over the course of the project.
b. Certainly, not all risks can be anticipated, but an effective risk management process can help to alleviate the effects of many unplanned events.
c. The students might first review the actions taken in this particular case. Once these have been reviewed, however, the instructor should encourage the students to apply these ideas to other project management cases. First, the consultant decided to conduct a performance test to determine if the project monitoring system would accurately reflect the project's progress and expenditures against the projected budget and schedule. The cost reporting system was simultaneously tested to verify that it would provide early warning discovery of any potential claim situations. An earned value, which depended on the stage of completion, was assigned to each work package so that the system was designed to measure the financial and physical completion of the project at any given time. A secondary budget curve was also prepared that looked into account contingencies by allocating them to each contract work package within the time frame they were most likely to occur. Since a majority of construction claims come from the electrical, mechanical, and architectural areas, special budget curves were established in these areas so that their associated work packages could be monitored more closely.

Additional Discussion Points:

The instructor may be interested in pursuing the issue of whether or not the problems cited in the case are the result of a faulty project management concept or the "risky" practices being used in construction projects. Taking it a step further, the instructor may wish to discuss the following question: If the project manager is correctly performing her job, is a third party consultant really needed? Finally, the entire case appears to boil down to the following question that could be discussed: Is the introduction of a third-party consultant truly a way to reduce risk or merely a way to pass that risk on to another party?

Controlling

5
CONTROLLING

Giving Mother Nature a Helping Hand 115

Managing Environmental Regulatory Approval Durations 117

Pittsburgh International Airport Midfield Terminal Energy Facility 121

Environmental Mega-Project under Way: Sludge Management in New York City 123

Gaining Project Acceptance 127

The Power of Politics: The Fourth Dimension of Managing the Large Public Project 131

The Environmental and Molecular Sciences Laboratory Project: Continuous Evolution in Leadership 135

Chrysler and Artemis: Striking Back with the Viper 137

St. Lucie Unit 2: A Nuclear Plant Built on Schedule 141

Measuring Successful Technical Performance: A Cost/Schedule/Technical Control System 145

The Legal Standards for "Prudent" Project Management 149

Giving Mother Nature a Helping Hand

C. Lewis Penland, C. Lewis Penland Inc.

PM Network, July 1994, pp. 14–22

SYNOPSIS

This case offers a short history of the game of golf and then describes the main issues to take into account when building or renovating a golf course. These include: materials, landscaping, and contractors. The case then covers the design, construction, and scheduling challenges of this type of project.

LEARNING OBJECTIVES

The students will observe the interdependency of the planning and execution processes in this construction project and how project management is a useful method for managing many kinds of endeavors. After reading the case and answering the questions presented, the students should become aware of:
- the vast number of stakeholders in a project
- the impact of planning in the final results of a project
- the different phases of a project and their importance
- the impact of technology on all projects.

DISCUSSION QUESTIONS AND POSSIBLE ANSWERS

1. List at least three stakeholders in a golf course design project and what they might have at stake in the project.
    a. The landowner/course owner—the investment in the course.
    b. The players—enjoyment of the course.
    c. Contracted constructor—the work and investment.
    d. The course designer—reputation, experience, investment.
    e. USGA—must approve and rate the course.
    f. Neighbors—Poor design could cause environmental hazard, or even a property hazard.
    g. Wildlife—Displace or change the ecology.
2. The *PMBOK Guide* established five phases of a project: initiating, planning, execution, controlling, and closing. In this case, most of the activities required for the development of a golf course are mentioned. Define each of the processes and identify at least two tasks for each of these process groups in golf course development.
    a. From the *PMBOK Guide*, section 3.2, Process Groups, the five processes are defined as: initiating process—recognizing that a project or phase should begin and committing to do so; planning process—devising and

maintaining a workable scheme to accomplish the business need that the project has undertaken to address; executing process—coordinating people and other resources to carry out a plan; controlling process—ensuring that project objectives are met by monitoring and measuring progress and taking corrective action when necessary; and closing process—formalizing acceptance of the project or phase and bringing it to an orderly end.

- *Initiating:* Having owners committed, making the resources available
- *Planning:* Design the course (landscaping), design the irrigation system, gather topographic maps, develop clear objective of a challenging and enjoyable course, develop estimates of materials, take into account the integration of original elements (animals, rocks, etc.)
- *Executing:* Construct the course, choose the turf, move material, the process of clearing the land, section of contractors, finish the shaping of the land with tractors, seed and sod the land, select materials for the greens, traps, and tee boxes
- *Controlling:* Verify the quality of materials, follow the schedule, verify the fulfillment of the initial requirements, follow-up with the contractors
- *Closing:* Final activities, opening day.

3. As a USGA course evaluator and stakeholder, what should your primary concern be?

   a. To communicate the rules and regulations of acceptable course design with the project managers. *PMBOK Guide,* Section 10.2, regarding information distribution, would be a good basis for the methods an evaluator could follow.

4. As the project manager on the renovation of the eighteenth hole at the famed Pebble Beach Golf Course, what is the most important aspect of your project from a personal standpoint?

   a. Scheduling—you are working on a very profitable course and any time the hole is being repaired means lost revenue for the course.
   b. Quality—you are working on one of the world's most famous courses and must assure the quality of the renovated hole.
   c. Reputation—by doing good work on this job, your reputation will grow and mean the chance for future employment and revenue.

5. The students are encouraged to do some research concerning the management and technology implications involved in the design, construction, and management of a golf course. A few references that provide useful insight into these matters include: *Golf Course Architecture: Design, Construction and Restoration Planning,* by Michael Hurdzan, Sleeping Bear Press, Chelsea, February, 1996; *Golf Course Management and Construction,* by Balogh, Lewis Publishers, June 1992; and *The Golf Course: Planning, Design, Construction and Management,* by F. W. Hawtree, Routledge, Chapman & Hall, Incorporated, New York, April 1983.

   a. The planning and design of the course will have a greater effect on the course than final construction because construction can always be repaired, but poor design would require rework of the entire project.
   b. Probable use of the court to include financial liability of the course.
   c. A plan for how the course will be used and maintained.

Managing Environmental Regulatory Approval Durations

Edward W. Ionata, PMP, Parsons Brinckerhoff

PMI *Proceedings*, 1993, pp. 152–56

Synopsis

This case describes the project of gaining permits, approvals, and licenses for two mega-projects in Boston, Massachusetts. These two projects: the Boston Harbor project and the Central Artery/Third Harbor Tunnel project required the acquisition of over four hundred permits. If the acquisition of these permits is not handled in a methodical manner, the process will become a bottleneck in the completion of the mega-projects. Through controls and coordination of the permitting processes and the use of project management, the permitting process can be scheduled and controlled effectively. This case serves as an example specifically for project scheduling management.

Learning Objectives

Through the study of this case, students will gain a better understanding as to the effects of seemingly peripheral activities in the completion of a project. Students should also gain a better understanding of:
- project scheduling management
- project integration management
- the management of complex projects
- using a schedule as a project control.

Discussion Questions and Possible Answers

1. What efforts were made to decrease complexity in the permitting process? How did these methods reduce the risk involved in the project?
   a. The complexity of the permitting process was reduced by having experienced permitting staff on hand to go over the work designs to ensure compliance with the permitting regulations.
   b. The complexity was also reduced by "packaging" work together for "packaged" permits, thus reducing the number of permits necessary to complete the work.
   c. Working to ease the permitting process served to reduce the risk of the project simply by decreasing the effects of or eliminating the permitting bottlenecks.
2. Project time management is a key factor on any project. The project described in the case was especially sensitive to any delay or any disapproval

of permits. In section 6, Project Time Management, the *PMBOK Guide* identifies five major activities to be carried out to ensure a prompt completion of the project. One of these factors is schedule development. Define the concept of schedule development and how it was carried out in this project.

   a. Schedule development, as defined by *PMBOK Guide*, section 6.4, is defined as analyzing activity sequences, activity durations, and resource requirements to create the project schedule. The activity was carried out by meeting with the appropriate agencies and determining what sequence was necessary for submitting permits, approximately how long the process would take, and which permits, avoiding redundancy, were required.

3. Another important activity in project time management is schedule control. Document the description of this activity and how it was undertaken in this project.

   a. Schedule control, as defined by *PMBOK Guide*, section 6.5, is concerned with influencing factors that create schedule changes to ensure that these changes are beneficial, determine that the schedule has changed, and managing the actual changes when and as they occur. This was achieved in the project by the close relationship with the permit agencies through meetings, a detailed schedule, and accurate permit status tracking. These steps eliminated the typical guesswork involved with any factor beyond the control of management.

4. How did this project incorporate project integration management (*PMBOK Guide*, chapter 4) in its process?

   a. The project managers worked to assure that the permit process agreed with the design and construction segments of the project. By developing, executing, and controlling the change, planning was able to stay integrated with the rest of the project and assure a smooth implementation.

5. Given that the governmental agencies all have an interest in the timely completion of this project, how can the project managers exploit this strategic issue in the completion of the project?

   a. The adequate management of this strategic issue will allow the project's management to work closely with the governmental agencies; project management can assure that bottlenecks such as the permit process can be expedited. By working with the government as stakeholders, this relationship will serve as favorable to the project management.

6. How important did project management consider the permitting process? Was this level of attention and concern appropriate?

   a. The permitting process was considered a key element and was treated as a project sub-plan, requiring that a work breakdown structure be created for the process.

   b. This level of attention was appropriate since permitting it is a bottleneck in the process of the entire project. Therefore, delays in the permit process meant delays for the entire project.

ADDITIONAL DISCUSSION POINTS:

Permits and other necessary relationships with governmental agencies are a regular activity in many projects. Delays and difficulties in these processes can mean additional costs and scheduling problems. This fact can generate ethical dilemmas for the project manager (i.e., looking for short-cuts). Students should read PMI's Code of Ethics for the Project Management Profession (see Appendix A) and discuss its impact on their work.

Pittsburgh International Airport Midfield Terminal Energy Facility

Philip J. Damiani, Manager, Mechanical Engineering; SE Technologies, Inc.
Robert J. Teachout, Senior Engineer, Mechanical Engineering; SE Technologies, Inc.

PMI *Proceedings* 1992, pp. 44–50

Synopsis

This case describes the process of selecting and designing the heating technology for the Midfield Terminal Energy Facility at the Pittsburgh International Airport. It also discusses the importance and impact of project management in carrying out this endeavor. The case compares the widely used steam heating system with a hot water system. The author highlights the importance of realistic scheduling, budgeting, equipment selection, quality adherence, and minimization of long-term costs.

Learning Objectives

After studying this case, the students will further understand the impact of the following issues of project management:
- negotiation
- the relationship between quality, costing/budgeting, and scheduling
- selection from a set of options
- project schedule management.

Discussion Questions and Possible Answers

1. The design team was concerned with developing "real" quotations and selecting the best energy system. Which of the nine project management body of knowledge areas was used most? Describe this process.
    a. Project cost management.
    b. This process is defined in *PMBOK Guide,* section 7, as "the processes required to ensure that the project is completed within the approved budget. It consists of resource planning, cost estimating, cost budgeting, and cost control." The approach used by the design team resembles a "life-cycle costing."

2. The authors state that project cost is directly proportional to the level of quality required. Comment on this statement.
    a. There is a relationship between cost and quality, but that relationship rarely is directly proportional. With proper scheduling and planning, as well as with proper control of the project, quality in the process is assured. This

is an important point, for the best equipment and materials purchased will not provide the best quality end product when the process used is faulty.

3. Something which was not mentioned by the authors of this case was that the airport was created using public funds and thus faced the problems associated with dealing with the government and consequently the public as stakeholders. How did the owner/engineers of this project deal with this challenge?

   a. Although not clearly discussed, the owner/engineers must have included the government in their development plans through meeting and other communications. By keeping the stakeholders informed and including them in the process when appropriate, the ownership the stakeholders grow to feel for the project ensures their support and cooperation.

4. The author states that if realistic budget and quality are established, the project is properly controlled by controlling the schedule. They later state that the schedule is the key controlling mechanism. What are the key assumptions of this statement?

   a. One of the assumptions is that the scope management process was properly carried out and that identified activities are clearly stated.
   b. The project will not face non-controllable factors that will create unplanned challenges (Risk evaluation).
   c. All the activities will have been scheduled for and their impact recognized.

5. The author mentions the importance of negotiating the quality, budgeting, and scheduling with the project's owner. Elements of every project and even every activity of life involve negotiation. Project managers always have to conduct negotiations in a project. What are some strategies for negotiating as a project manager?

   a. In the book, *Project Management: Strategic Design and Implementation*, 2nd ed., by Cleland, Chapter 15, A Project Manager's Guide To Contracting, describes the negotiating process. This method is presented in the book, *Getting to Yes: Negotiating Agreement Without Giving In*, by Roger Fisher and William Ury. This straightforward, creative strategy for firmly pursuing your interests and dealing with interests conflicting with yours, has four main principles:
   - Separate people from the problems.
   - Focus on the common interests in the process rather than the opposing positions of the parties.
   - Generate a number of creative options prior to beginning negotiation.
   - Insist that results be based on some objective criteria.

ADDITIONAL DISCUSSION POINTS:

The author mentions that "many owners try to save money by minimizing engineering costs and that this often results in poor construction documents and excessive contingencies in the form of additional construction change orders to a project." Have the students divide into two groups and have one of the groups defend the importance of planning and the other group defend the importance of monitoring ongoing processes.

Environmental Mega-Project under Way: Sludge Management in New York City

Itzhak Wirth, St. John's University

PMI *Proceedings*, 1993, pp. 666–80

Synopsis

This case describes the city of New York program to implement land-base alternatives to ocean disposal of sludge from its water pollution control plants. The project will guarantee the complement of the Ocean Dumping Ban Act. The case offers a fair amount of background and describes in detail the use of the work breakdown structure, and the process followed in the alternative selection for the short, intermediate, and long-term solutions. The author also examines some aspects of the project against concepts and definitions from the *PMBOK Guide*.

Learning Objectives

Through the study of this case, students should gain a better understanding of:
- the work breakdown structure
- the project life-cycle
- project cost management
- environmental projects.

Discussion Questions and Possible Answers

1. The author presents the work breakdown structure of the project in detail and explains the process followed in its development. *PMBOK Guide*, section 5.3.2, Tool and Techniques for Scope Definition, discusses methods used to develop a work breakdown structure. Which of those methods listed were used in the case?

    a. *PMBOK Guide* identifies two main techniques: work breakdown structure templates and decomposition. "Decomposition involves subdividing the major project deliverables into smaller, more manageable components until deliverables are defined in sufficient detail to support future project activities." Therefore, this project was based on decomposition when the major deliverables of the project (level one) are broken down to levels three and four with the purpose of obtaining smaller, manageable components.

2. Would you consider this case the description of one or three projects, given the three distinct phases described and the extended time frame for the phases described?
   a. This project should be considered one project with three interrelated phases. This is in part because the phases cannot stand on their own in terms of scheduling, cost, or procurement management. Also, there is a described life-cycle for the project as a whole, describing the end of the entire project. In all, it is best to consider the three phases one since the management of the project was developed for all three phases.
3. The team work package is mentioned near the end of the case. It seems to be a synonym of the work categories described in the case. Define a work package and describe any similarities between the two terms.
   a. The *PMBOK Guide* glossary definition of work package is "a deliverable at the lowest level of the work breakdown structure. A work package may be divided into activities." From this definition and the work breakdown structure presented in this case, project categories refer to Level 2 in the case where they are further divided into tasks and subtasks. Therefore, the two terms do not have the same meaning.
4. This project doesn't mention cost management, aside from estimating costs for each phase and describing the costing elements in the work breakdown structure. In light of the described penalties for noncompliance with the dumping bans, how important is cost management?
   a. Given the length of the project and its possible high profile in New York City, cost management would be very important. But in the *PMBOK Guide* description of resource planning, Section 7.1, the major steps of creating a work breakdown structure, gathering historical information, creating a scope statement, and essentially making an evaluation of the infrastructure necessary for the successful completion of the project have all been completed. Thus, significant steps have been made in working for the cost management of the project.
5. The case states that there is not a section in the *PMBOK Guide* which directly addresses the site selection process. Is it possible that all of the sections of the *PMBOK Guide* at least generally describe this process? Go through each section and describe how it might affect the site selection process.
   - *Project Integration:* Developing the plan for site selection.
   - *Scope Management:* Planning how many sites will be evaluated.
   - *Time Management:* Developing the activities necessary for selecting a site
   - *Cost Management:* Determining the resources available to create a site.
   - *Quality Management:* Determining how much control over the site will be possible.
   - *Human Resource Management:* Planning the relations between sites.
   - *Communications Management:* Communicating the environmental risk to site stakeholders.
   - *Risk Management:* Determining the environmental risk of a site.
   - *Procurement Management:* Purchasing the site.

ADDITIONAL DISCUSSION POINTS:

The case states that there are not any references to project marketing in the *PMBOK Guide.* Have the students discuss any guidelines that they think would be appropriate for a section on project marketing for the *PMBOK Guide.*

Have the students research the topic of a work breakdown structure and make a brief report on its main purpose, the purpose it serves, and its strengths and weaknesses.

Gaining Project Acceptance

Larry Martin, Vice President and Director of Transportation Environmental Analysis, CH2M Hill
Paula Green, Environmental Coordinator, District IV Illinois DOT

Civil Engineering, August 1995, pp. 51–53

SYNOPSIS

This case describes a process followed to gain project acceptance in two transportation projects in Illinois. The authors present five essential elements of any project with high community impact. The case stress the importance of involving the stakeholders and addressing their concerns early in the project development in order to avoid resistance and adversities in the future.

LEARNING OBJECTIVES

After developing the case, the students will gain a greater understanding of:
- how to deal with stakeholders
- the myriad type of stakeholders
- stakeholders' power
- the wide range of project challenges.

DISCUSSION QUESTIONS AND POSSIBLE ANSWERS

1. What is a "stakeholder?"
    a. O. Kharbanda and J. Pinto, *Successful Project Managers: Leading Your Team to Success,* Chapter 2, Stakeholder Analysis and Project Management, state: "An organizational 'stakeholder' refers to any individual or group that has an active stake in the activities of the organization."
    b. *PMBOK Guide,* Section 2.2, Project Stakeholders: "Project stakeholders are individuals and organizations who are actively involved in the project, or whose interests may be positively or negatively affected as a result of project execution or successful project competition."

2. Regardless of the size of the endeavor, every project has to deal with stakeholders. Develop a list of the most common stakeholders on any project.
    a. O. Kharbanda and J. Pinto, *Successful Project Managers: Leading Your Team to Success,* Chapter 2, Stakeholder Analysis and Project Management, suggest that the project manager has to address two types of stakeholders: internal and external ones. Internal stakeholders include: top management, accountants, functional managers, and employees. External stakeholders include: clients, competitors, suppliers, and environmental, political, and intervention groups.

b. *PMBOK Guide*, Section 2.2, Project Stakeholders, presents as key stakeholders of every project: project manager, customer (final user of the result of the project), team members and their families, government agencies, media, lobbying organizations, individual citizens, and society at large.

3. The method used by the Hearth of Illinois project to gain project acceptance has five key elements. List and define those elements.

   a. The five elements and their definitions are:
      - *Identifying Stakeholders:* Through this process the project identifies all groups or individuals with a stake in the project. The process included going to the area, visiting adjacent institutions, businesses, houses, and local representatives and with their help identifying "who cares about this project."
      - *Tiering Approach:* This approach was used due to the physical impossibility of holding a meeting with all the stakeholders simultaneously. Input or approval from different types of stakeholders is solicited at different stages of the project.
      - *Identifying Issues:* The project should clearly establish its scope, allowing stakeholders to see how they are really affected by the project. Then the project manager must listen to their concerns.
      - *Resolution:* In this phase the project plans are adjusted to meet stakeholders' concerns. Additionally meetings are held to guarantee the consideration of the concerns in the plans.
      - *Formal Approval:* Thanks to the previous four steps, this phase is almost free of negative surprises. This process proceeds with the final launching of the project plan. The infrastructure developed will help the project through its life.

4. Consider any of the other cases found in this casebook. Identify all the internal and external stakeholders for the project and briefly discuss their stakes. List any strategic issues that could inhibit the progress on the project.

   a. Answers to this question will vary depending on the case selected by the student. Most of the projects in this casebook lend themselves readily to a stakeholder analysis.

5. Define a generic procedure for stakeholder analysis.

   a. In his article, Project Stakeholder Management, *Project Management Journal*, September 1986, pp. 36–43, David I. Cleland presents a model of the project stakeholder management process. In this model seven stages are suggested:
      - identify stakeholders
      - gather information on stakeholders
      - determine stakeholder strengths and weaknesses
      - identify stakeholder strategy
      - predict stakeholder behavior
      - implement stakeholder strategy.

      The activities that should be done under each of these stages is further described by Cleland in this article.

ADDITIONAL DISCUSSION POINTS:

Today, public and private projects are more sensitive to public opinion and pressure from external groups. The students can work in groups and present a case in which they were involved or that they have read about where the influence of stakeholders influenced the original outcome of the project.

The Power Of Politics: The Fourth Dimension of Managing the Large Public Project

Bud Baker, Wright State University
Raj Menon, Wright State University

PMI Canada *Proceedings*, 1994, pp. 830–33

Synopsis

This paper discusses the role of politics in large public projects and how these can influence the success or failure of a project. The author examines the interstate highway system and the superconducting supercollider projects in detail from political and public relations perspectives. The case develops general advice for the management of large public endeavors.

Learning Objectives

After answering the questions, the students will gain a deeper understanding of:
- project critical success factors
- project stakeholders
- large public projects
- the power of politics.

Discussion Questions and Possible Answers

1. Besides politics there are numerous other factors that play a role in the success or failure of a project. Identify five to six of those elements and discuss the most critical among them.

   a. From O. Kharbanda and J. Pinto in *Successful Project Managers: Leading Your Team to Success*, Chapter 4, Project Critical Success Factors, identify the following critical success factors:
   - *Project Mission*. Including clearly defined goals and general directions.
   - *Top Management Support*. Willingness of top management to provide the necessary resources and authority/power for implementation success.
   - *Schedule Plan*. A detailed specification of the individual action steps for system implementation.
   - *Client Consultation*. Communication, consultation, and active listening to all parties impacted by the proposed project.

- *Personnel.* Recruitment, selection, and training of the necessary personnel for the implementation project team.
- *Technical Tasks.* Availability of the required technology and expertise to accomplish the specific technical action steps to bring the project online.
- *Client Acceptance.* The act of "selling" the final product to its ultimate intended users.
- *Monitoring and Feedback.* Timely provision of comprehensive control information at each stage in the implementation process.
- *Communication.* The provision of an appropriate network and necessary data to all key actors in the project implementation process.
- *Troubleshooting.* Ability to handle unexpected crises and deviations from the plan.

From a research project that that looked at over 400 projects and tried to assess the importance of the ten factors, Pinto and Slevin identified the mission as the most important factor in the study.

2. The paper states that the interstate highway system project was successful because, among other factors, "the act offered something to everyone, and aroused the ire of almost no one." The statement clearly refers to the project stakeholders. Develop a list of the common stakeholders of any project.

   a. O. Kharbanda and J. Pinto in *Successful Project Managers: Leading Your Team to Success*, Chapter 2, Stakeholder Analysis and Project Management, suggest that the project manager has to address two types of stakeholders: internal and external ones. Internal stakeholders include: top management, accountants, functional managers, and other employees. External stakeholders include: clients, competitors, suppliers, and environmental, political, and "interventor" groups.

   b. *PMBOK Guide*, Section 2.2, Project Stakeholders, presents as key stakeholders of every project: project manager, customer (final user of the result of the project), team members and their families, government agencies, media, lobbying organizations, individual citizens, and society at large.

3. What does the author mean by "the fourth dimension of managing?"

   a. Baker expands his discussion of "the fourth dimension of project management" in Political Strategies for Projects and Project Managers, (Cleland, David I., editor, *Field Guide to Project Management*). He states that "Astute project managers accept and understand the importance of politics as a key success factor in their efforts." He also lists and discusses six aspects of politics to consider in project management including active listening, project structure, coalitions building, dealing with government, setting expectations, and communicating with all stakeholders.

4. Aside from the superconducting supercollider, there are other examples of large projects that were terminated primarily because of political considerations. From your own experience or the literature find and discuss another example with the class. What could have prevented the termination of the project?

   a. Examples will vary but the discussion of prevention methods should focus on the six key factors cited in the instructor notes for question 3.

ADDITIONAL DISCUSSION POINTS:

The case concludes with four main lessons learned from the analysis of the interstate highway project and the superconducting supercollider project. In small groups, students should list and discuss specific actions to implement these lessons. The instructor may want to select a particular case to apply the lessons or use generalizations.

The Environmental and Molecular Sciences Laboratory Project: Continuous Evolution in Leadership

D.E. Knutson, PMP
J.K. McClusky, Pacific Northwest Laboratory

PMI Canada *Proceedings*, 1994, pp. 923–29

Synopsis

This case describes the United States (U.S.) Department of Energy (DOE) effort in the development of an environmental and molecular science laboratory to treat toxic waste. The authors give a strong background on the project; they also stress the needs the project addresses and the benefits derived from the endeavor. The case depicts the integration process between DOE and the project management team, as well as the innovative planning and control process for the scientific research.

Learning Objectives

From this environmental government project, the students will enhance their understanding of:
- the mission and objective purposes
- the matrix organization
- scope management
- working with the government.

Discussion Questions and Possible Answers

1. The author highlights the importance of having a clear mission and objectives in the project. What does it mean to have a project with a clear mission and objectives?

    a. O. Kharbanda and J. Pinto in *Successful Project Managers: Leading Your Team to Success*, Chapter 4, Project Critical Success Factors, state that the most influential factor in the success of a project is its mission. They describe a clear mission as the process of communicating the goals, scope, and impact of the project to all the stakeholders and especially to team members and future customers. They also emphasize the importance of project team members' support of the mission.

2. The case also mentions the importance of scope management in a research environment. Define scope management for any project.
    a. *PMBOK Guide* Chapter 5, Project Scope Management, states: "Project Scope Management includes the processes required to ensure that the project includes all the work required, and only the work required, to complete the project successfully. It is primarily concerned with defining and controlling what is or is not included in the project."
3. The relocation process was carried out very successfully and only meant 2 percent over cost. To which factor do you attribute this accomplishment?
    a. The project team built a very close relationship with all the agencies (stakeholders) involved in the process. These relationships and the proper use of project management allowed them to minimize the impact of the relocation process.
4. The author states: "The challenge that the EMSL project met was to define the capabilities of EMSL in a way that identified their relevant application, fundamental need, and feasibility of completion in a way that could be understood and accepted." What would be some of the consequences of not defining the capabilities in this way?
    a. The most important and obvious consequence would be the loss of stakeholder support for the project, without which the project might be terminated.
5. The author states: "A matrix organization consisting of personnel drawn from 11 research, technical, and support organizations was created to handle the myriad technical, regulatory, and documentation efforts of the project." Discuss the advantages and disadvantages of the matrix organization.
    a. Advantages include the use of dedicated project team members, provision of a "home" for project personnel between assignments, efficient allocation of personnel, specialization of personnel, organizational flexibility, etc.
    b. Disadvantages include difficulties of implementation, dual-reporting situations that may cause conflicts, competing priorities of project personnel, etc.
    c. The instructor may also wish to relate or have students relate personal experience with a matrix organization.

ADDITIONAL DISCUSSION POINTS:

This case focuses on proper scope management. The instructor may wish to present the students with a sample project and ask the students to develop a scope statement that might be used to manage the project.

Chrysler and Artemis: Striking Back with the Viper

Stephen W.T. O'Keeffe

Industrial Engineering, December 1994, pp. 15–17

Synopsis

Chrysler needed to change the way it was bringing products to the market. Facing tight deadlines, myriad variables, and working with finite resources required the use of project management. The case describes how Chrysler was able to achieve its goal successfully and stresses the role of the use of project management software (Artemis Prestige) in the process.

Learning Objectives

After the discussion of this case, the students will gain a further understanding of:
- project management software
- the project life-cycle
- the wide applicability of project management
- project's schedule.

Discussion Questions and Possible Answers

1. Chrysler had to shorten its product introduction cycles in order to be competitive in the automotive industry. What are the general characteristics of a project life-cycle?

    a. *PMBOK Guide,* Section 2.1.2, Characteristics of the Project Life Cycle, states: "Most project life-cycle descriptions share a number of common characteristics:

    Cost and staffing levels are low at the start, higher toward the end, and drop rapidly as the project draws to a conclusion.

    The probability of successful completion of the project is lowest, and hence risk and uncertainty are highest, at the start of the project. The probability of successful completion generally gets progressively higher as the project continues.

    The ability of the stakeholders to influence the final characteristics of the project product and the final cost of the project is highest at the start and gets progressively lower as the project continues. A major contributor to this phenomenon is that the cost of changes and error correction generally increases as the project continues.

Although many project life-cycles have similar phase names with similar work products required, few are identical."

2. Discuss the competitive advantages of reducing product development times in the automobile industry and other industries.

   a. This discussion should focus on the importance of "speed to market" in today's global, competitive markets. There is no question that product development times have been shortened in many industries and that in order to remain competitive, companies must keep up with the pace. Typically, the company that gets to market first may gain the largest market share and enhance product profitability—but if the product is successful, competitors will move in!

   b. The instructor might continue the discussion by having students relate personal experiences with being first or not being first to the market with a particular product. Other discussion points on this issue might include the kinds of products involved when it may not be advantageous to be first in the market.

3. The management of the project was able to analyze various scenarios through the use of the "what if" feature of the software. What are the key elements to take into account in developing a project's schedule?

   a. *PMBOK Guide*, Section 6.4.1, Inputs to Schedule Development, identifies the following elements:
      - "*Project Network Diagram* is a schematic display of the project's activities and the logical relationships (dependencies) among them.
      - *Activity Duration Estimating* involves assessing the number of work periods likely to be needed to complete each identified activity.
      - *Resource Requirements* is a description of what type of resources are required and in what quantities for each element of the work breakdown structure. The resources will be obtained either through staff acquisition or procurement.
      - *Resource Pool Description.* Knowledge of what resources will be available at what times and in what patterns is necessary for schedule development.
      - *Calendars.* Project and resource calendars identify periods when work is allowed.
      - *Constraints* are factors that will limit the project management team options.
      - *Assumptions* are factors that, for planning purposes, will be consider to be true, real, or certain. Assumptions generally involve a degree of risk and will normally be an output of risk identification.
      - *Leads and Lags.* Any of the dependencies may require specification of a lead or a lag in order to accurately define the relationship."

4. Explain the advantages that Artemis (the project management software) brought to the Viper project. How did these advantages contribute to a shorter product development time for Viper?

   a. The tool allowed management to "see the big picture and to gauge the impact of each operation on that panoramic view." It also gave the team the opportunity to perform "what ifs" and do effective risk management. This let them "recognize those processes that most needed attention, and to identify where resource redistribution could have the greatest impact on net yield." The software aided in the ability to reduce both time and cost elements of the project. This case illustrates that one of the primary keys to the success of the Viper project was effective time and cost management through the use of a project management software tool.

ADDITIONAL DISCUSSION POINTS:

Chrysler chose Artemis Prestige (Lucas Management Systems) as its project management software. The instructor may wish to ask students to research on other packages available in the market, their main features, applications and costs.

A.B. Badiru and P.S. Pulat in *Comprehensive Project Management,* Appendix E: Project Management Software, give a general description of the software available.

St Lucie Unit 2: A Nuclear Plant Built on Schedule

W. B. Derrickson, Director of Projects, Florida Power & Light Company

PMI *Proceedings*, 1983, pp. V-E-1–V-E-14

Synopsis

This case discusses the general project management practices that enabled the construction of a nuclear power plant to be completed on time and within budget. Florida Power and Light (FPL) has four nuclear power plants in operation. St. Lucie Unit 2 was the last to go operational. Work began on the St. Lucie 2 nuclear power plant back in 1971. The full power license for the St. Lucie Unit 2 was granted by the Nuclear Regulatory Commission (NRC) on June 10, 1983, only six years after construction had started. This was done despite the issuance of a number of regulations by the NRC, a 1979 hurricane which did considerable damage to the Reactor Auxiliary Building and some labor problems that were encountered.

Learning Objectives

This case will provide the students with some issues to consider when devising a project control system. The students will also become aware of the need to design a control system that not only satisfies the needs of project management, but also fits well into the organization. After discussing the case, the students should understand the following points:
- some of the various ways to structure a project control system
- the importance of constructing a control system that is based on the needs of the project, the benefits to be gained, and the resulting costs
- the advantages of having a program that reinforces the establishment of project goals and ways to measure the progress toward those goals
- the usefulness of additional quality and performance indicators.

Discussion Questions and Possible Answers

1. Describe the project planning and scheduling system used on the St. Lucie Unit 2 project. Define schedule control.
    a. Over a period of six months, a team of construction supervisors devised the master project schedule covering the entire project duration, a period of over sixty-five months. This schedule consisted of an integrated engineering and construction plan along with a summary of the start-up logic to be used. As a part of this scheduling process, all of the major milestones were identified and the subsequent dates determined. This master project schedule laid the foundation for all future planning.

b. *PMBOK Guide,* Section 6.5, Schedule Control, defines schedule control as: "Schedule control is concern with (a) influencing the factors which create schedule changes to ensure that changes are beneficial, (b) determining that the schedule has changed, and (c) managing the actual changes when and as they occur. Schedule control must be thoroughly integrated with the other control processes."

2. What are some of the key issues to consider when evaluating the usefulness and effectiveness of a project control system?

   a. It is important for the student to recognize the need to evaluate any project monitoring and control system in terms of its usefulness and the advantages it will offer. This must also be weighed against the resources that will be consumed to accomplish the monitoring and control. In this particular case, the various levels of reporting may be based on past experience of nuclear plant construction. With its past successful performance record it would be hard to dispute that the system was appropriate for its needs. The students still must understand the need to evaluate the practicality of their methods and procedures before trying to transfer them into another project management environment.

   b. It is not clear where the work breakdown structure fits into this planning scheme. This is further confused by the definition of a "work package" as being the work performed in a specific cubicle. Is there a true overall structure to this work division? No mention is made of trying to assign the work activities to specific individuals. The plan appears to rely on general indicators that serve to point out problems so that the managers can in turn designate a project team member to take the necessary corrective action. Does each one of the schedule levels serve a specific and useful purpose or is there some redundancy? Based on the descriptions, there does seem to be some redundancy. The problem is that with all of these different "levels" one may lose sight of the fact that all of the schedules are interrelated and changes in one will affect the others.

   c. H. Kerzner in *Project Management: A Systems Approach to Planning, Scheduling, and Controlling,* Chapter 5, Management Functions, states that an adequate control system considers three phases: measuring, evaluating, and correcting, and defines each as follows: "Measuring: determining through formal and informal reports the degree to which progress toward objectives is being made. Evaluating: determining causes of and possible ways to act on significant deviations from planned performance. Correcting: taking action to correct an unfavorable trend or take advantage of an unusually favorable trend."

3. Describe some of the scope management factors that contributed to the success of the project.

   a. In 1977, FPL made the successful completion (i.e., on time and within budget) of the St. Lucie 2 project as an organizational objective. Since FPL uses a management by objectives program, all of the departments were required to establish their own objectives that would contribute to this overall corporate goal. Consequently, the importance of the project was emphasized throughout the entire organization.

   b. The project team decided to place special priority on the engineering, design and delivery of piping and hangars. In fact, they were scheduled for a full eighteen months before the early start dates. As a result, the hangar installation was able to precede the pipe erection thereby reducing the need for the use of temporary pipe support. The project team performed a detailed review of the design of St. Lucie 1 in order to recommend ways that the design could be improved. Although not mentioned in the case, it would also be extremely beneficial to review the various project management techniques that were employed in order to assess their usefulness while also examining the problems they encountered.

4. Describe how the management assessment of performance and quality (MAPQ) was performed.

    a. Two surveys were administered to top management in an attempt to get them to determine the project's objectives and some possible indicators for these objectives. In addition, key personnel were interviewed to determine other performance and quality indicators that could be used to develop goals or targets for each objective. Next, management by objective/indicator charts were prepared that displayed past and future goals. One individual was assigned the responsibility for the progress of each chart and for having a management review system in place using management-by-exception principles.

5. How does the MAPQ process assist the scope management function?

    a. The whole process reinforces the concept of defining project goals. Since projects are the vehicles for executing organizational strategies, top management should have already determined the project goals during its project selection process. Now, this program forces them to review those goals and officially convey them to the lower levels of management. It gets both top management and other key project personnel involved in developing measures or quality indicators that are linked to the project's goals and can be used to assess the progress toward those goals. Using these indicators as a basis, milestones or targeted levels can be set that will ensure the attainment of the overall objectives. Through the measurement of the performance indicators, management will be kept informed on how well it is meeting the project goals. In addition, the system will alert the management to potential problem areas that might have otherwise gone undetected.

    b. The students should understand that this program merely supplements the project management system by providing additional information in such areas as productivity, reliability, and quality assurance. It is not designed as a replacement for the traditional project control system that emphasizes the cost and budget of the project.

ADDITIONAL DISCUSSION POINTS:

The instructor may want to go into greater detail on why this nuclear construction project turned out to be a success in a trouble-ridden industry. The instructor might also consider discussing the various charts and graphs depicted toward the end of the case. Finally, the instructor could elaborate on the organizational culture that must exist in order to stimulate employees to look for possible technical innovations or better ways of doing things.

Measuring Successful Technical Performance: A Cost/Schedule/Technical Control System

Robert H. Kohrs, Program Manager, Underwater Tests, Westinghouse Electric Corporation
Gordon C. Weingarten, Programs Business Manager, Westinghouse Electric Corporation

PMI Canada *Proceedings*, 1986, pp. 158–64

Synopsis

This case details an approach for measuring technical success. Availability of cost and schedule control systems are discussed and the lack of quantifying technical performance is expressed. Background of the authors' work is given and schedule and cost variances are explained. A cost plus incentive format, with incentives on cost, schedule, and technical performance prompted the development of a process for measuring technical performance. This process is detailed and described for a hypothetical case.

Learning Objectives

The objectives to be met in discussion of this case include:
- understanding the process for measuring the technical performance parameter of a project
- examining the interdependence between cost, schedule, and technical performance factors
- identifying the variances associated with cost, schedule, and technical performance
- recognizing how incentive contracting helped to improve and measure technical performance in this case.

Discussion Questions and Possible Answers

1. Demonstrate your understanding of the project manager's triangle as presented in the case.
    a. The project manager's triangle consists of three performance factors: cost, schedule, and technical. Balancing and coordinating these factors is critical. Maximization of one factor may result in inefficiencies in the other two.

2. How can cost and schedule variances be measured? Discuss the difficulties in defining technical variance.
   a. Cost variance is measured by comparing actual cost with budgeted using existing financial reports. Key milestones are defined in project plans. Schedule variance is the difference between actual milestone completion and planned milestone completion. It is difficult to measure the success or failure of a technical task. Quantifying technical performance is not as common or discussed as frequently in the literature as measuring cost and schedule performance.
   b. The foundation for measuring technical performance should be based on determining what the customer needs, wants, and expects. That is, successful technical performance is directly dependent on customer satisfaction.
3. A successful project is one that not only fulfills the constraints of time, cost, and technical performance but fulfills other requirements such as minimal scope change and customer acceptance. Discuss some of these other requirements.
   a. Research in Kerzner, *Project Management: A Systems Approach to Planning, Scheduling, and Controlling*, as paraphrased, shows that a successful project is one that is completed:
      1. within the allocated time period,
      2. within the cost budget,
      3. at the specified performance level,
      4. with acceptance by the customer/user,
      5. with minimum or mutually agreed upon scope changes,
      6. without disturbing the primary work of the organization, and
      7. without altering the corporate culture.
4. The case emphasizes the importance of measuring technical performance. What are the elements to consider in performance reporting in cost, schedule, or technical performance?
   a. *PMBOK Guide*, section 10.3, Performance Reporting, states: "Performance reporting involves collecting and disseminating performance information in order to provide stakeholders with information about how resources are being used to achieve project objectives. This process includes:
      - Status reporting—describing where the project now stands.
      - Progress reporting—describing what the project team has accomplished.
      - Forecasting—predicting future project status and progress.
      - Performance reporting should generally provide information on scope, schedule, cost, and quality. Many projects also require information on risk and procurement. Reports may be prepared comprehensively or on an exception basis."

ADDITIONAL DISCUSSION POINTS:

Topics which can be discussed within the realm of cost control include: variance analysis (cost variance, schedule/performance, variance since last period, etc.), monitoring actual versus budgeted, and progress analysis. The instructor may discuss these topics in more detail with the class.

The students might also describe a project from their own work or school experience and apply the variance reporting model discussed in the case. They should list the incentive parameters and prepare summary variance report forms.

The Legal Standards for "Prudent" Project Management

Randall L. Speck, Rogovin, Huge & Lenzner, P.C.

PMI *Proceedings*, 1987, pp. 566–76

Synopsis

This article discusses the handling of several court cases involving allowances for recovery of project costs in utility rates. The cases attempt to judge the reasonableness of or "prudent" project management. The author describes the context for challenges to the reasonableness of project management, the standards for prudent project management, the burden of proving imprudence, substantive standards for prudent project management, and the calculation of imprudent project costs. Examples of each of these are given from various rate cases.

Learning Objectives

One of the aspects of the quality assurance division of quality management is formative quality evaluation, that is, conformance to external and internal standards, codes, contracts, policies, etc. Prudent project management defines the quality of the management process itself with respect to the reasonableness and conformance to acceptable standards. The instructor should concentrate on the following objectives for reviewing this particular case:
- understanding the definition of prudent project management
- recognizing why this concept has become important (i.e., the context for challenges to the reasonableness of project management)
- understanding the various standards, established in recent court cases, for prudent project management
- identifying what project managers can do, up front, to ensure that prudence can be demonstrated if need be
- discussing the three critical areas of prudence: planning, organization, and control
- understanding how the courts might calculate and disallow imprudent project costs.

Discussion Questions and Possible Answers

1. This case illustrates the importance and difficulty of cost estimating. What are some ways of estimating costs?
    a. *PMBOK Guide,* section 7.2.2, Tools and Techniques for Cost Estimating, explains the following three methods:

- Analogous Estimating: Also called top-down estimating, means using the actual cost of a previous, similar project as the basis for estimating the cost of the current project.
- Parametric Modeling: Parametric modeling involves using project characteristics (parameters) in a mathematical model to predict project costs. Models may be simple or complex.
- Bottom-up Estimating: This technique involves estimating the cost of individual work times, then summarizing or rolling up the individual estimates to get a project cost.

2. What is meant by "prudent" project management? How does this concept relate to quality management? Why has it become so important?

   a. This term has various definitions based on the numerous standards used to evaluate it; however, in general it refers to the reasonableness of the project management process with respect to conformance to cost, time, and technical performance objectives. Quality management includes formative quality evaluation which is the conformance to external legal and regulatory codes/standards and internal contracts, specifications, policies, and procedures. Prudent project management refers to the quality of the project management process itself. It has become an important topic because of the many recent court decisions which disallowed utilities to include cost overruns in their rates.

3. Discuss the various standards, established in court cases, for prudent project management. These include the reasonable project manager (reasonable person, community, standards, etc.), reasonable project management "under the circumstances," project managers' responsibility for vendor's actions, and "efficient" project management. What are some of the advantages and disadvantages of each of these tests of prudence?

   a. Students should be able to give a general understanding of the various kinds of standards which the courts might use to judge the prudence of project management. Advantages and disadvantages are listed in the case.

4. What can project managers do, up front, to ensure that proof of prudence can be given if need be? Discuss this in terms of the three critical areas: planning, organization, and control.

   a. Documentation and record keeping are the most important areas that should be addressed for prudent project management. The ability to demonstrate the specific causes for major cost increases is important. Project managers must be sure to use state-of-the-art planning techniques and establish a baseline plan. Clear responsibility, accountability, and authority should be established and roles must be defined for each project team member. Finally, proper control systems and milestone reporting must be done.

   b. The *PMBOK Guide* is an excellent model to use as a standard for prudent project management.

ADDITIONAL DISCUSSION POINTS:

The instructor might wish to get the students involved in a discussion of moral issues with respect to prudent project management (i.e., with respect to safety in the nuclear and other industries). This discussion might be related to PMI's Code of Ethics for the Project Management Profession (see Appendix A) and other professional ethical standards.

The instructor might also wish to discuss the article by David I. Cleland, Prudent and Reasonable Project Management, *Project Management Journal*, December 1995, pp. 90–97.

General

6
GENERAL

Communicating Constraints: Schedule Baseline and Recovery Measures on the Hong Kong Airport Projects   157

Can We Talk?: Communications Management for the Waste Isolation Pilot Plant, a Complex Nuclear Waste Management Project   159

The Demise of the Superconducting Supercollider: Strong Politics or Weak Management   163

Boeing Spares Distribution Center: A World-Class Facility Achieved through Partnering   167

Responding to the Northridge Earthquake   171

A Town Makes History by Rising to New Heights   173

Real-World Challenges to a Multinational Project Team: Building a Manufacturing Facility in India   175

Total Quality Management and Project Management   179

Organization and Management of a Multi-Organizational Single Responsibility Project   183

Prudent and Reasonable Project Management   187

The Space Shuttle Challenger Incident   191

Communicating Constraints: Schedule Baseline and Recovery Measures on the Hong Kong Airport Projects

Jhan Schmitz, International Bechtel Incorporated

PMI *Proceedings*, 1995, pp. 121–28

Synopsis

This case describes the Hong Kong Airport core program, a $20.4 billion (United States' dollars) project. The author provides a report on the development of the project as of the second quarter of 1995 and discusses the scheduling, stakeholder, procurement, and political challenges which the project is facing. The case gives a background description of the project and analyzes ten of its subprojects. The author also describes the management methodology and conflict resolution techniques applied to meet the administrative challenges found in the project.

Learning Objectives

Through this case, the students will be able to explore the importance of using project management in mega-projects, the relations between different components of huge projects, dealing with complex governmental agencies, and the "top-down/bottom-up" management methodology. From the discussion of this case, the students should better understand:
- a project organization
- the impact of control/schedule management
- the importance of the scope definition
- the management of a very complex and international project.

Discussion Questions and Possible Answers

1. What are the main objectives of this project?

    a. To manage the overall project to include the ten subprojects with the 200 contractors sponsored by four different sources on time within budget, meeting technical objectives mindful of the political constraints.

2. The Hong Kong Airport core project (ACP) is one of the largest projects undertaken in the late Twentieth Century. It is made up of several segments, each of which could itself be considered a major project. What kind of organizational structure is used in this project? How does the job of project manager differ from that of the entire ACP project and one of the segments?

a. An example of this projectized organizational structure is depicted in Figure 2-8 in the PMBOK, section 2.3.3, Organizational Structure, where each project manager has his own organization and responds to a chief executive. In many ways there would be little difference in project manager jobs. The project manager for the ACP project must coordinate all of the segments and assure that their schedules coordinate just as a segment project manager must assure that the project adheres to the schedule for her project. The only significant difference is the level of complexity of tasks on which the project managers must focus, for example, handling the political aspects of the project and coordination of all of the subprojects.

3. Explain the "top down/bottom up" management methodology described in the case. Relate this to the scope management of the project.

   a. The methodology described can to be directly related to the scope definition of the *PMBOK Guide*, section 5, specifically, section 5.3, Scope Definition, defined as subdividing the major project deliverables into smaller manageable components, and 5.4, Scope Verification, which is defined as formalized acceptance of the scope. This is described in the case study as establishing program level objectives, getting these endorsed by the proper agencies, and setting these as targets for the project segments.

4. The method for physical progress measurement is detailed in the case. This method allows for all segments of the project to be aggregated for an overall project measurement of project completion. How does this method differ from the *PMBOK Guide*, Chapter 6, Project Time Management, methods, and why do these difference exist?

   a. The methods used by the ACP project managers allow for a gross level completion analysis by looking at individual project status and not task status. Because of the size of the ACP project, activities and tasks cannot be individually linked on the project level, except on a very detailed level. However, the methods described in the *PMBOK Guide* can be used for the subprojects and the general methods for schedule control described: updates, corrective actions, and lessons learned.

5. Why must this project be managed from a change control/schedule perspective?

   a. It is necessary to monitor the influential factors as described in *PMBOK Guide*, section 4.3, Overall Change Control. This is done in order to create the necessary changes in the project to guarantee the schedule, making sure that the deliverables are on time despite influencing factors. Specifically, if this is not done we will see increasing costs, delays in the interrelated projects, and political conflict and thus great difficulties throughout the ACP project. An example of this is the problem which was faced when the electrical power project was behind schedule and other projects requiring that power were affected.

ADDITIONAL DISCUSSION POINTS:

This project has an important role in the Sino-British relationship regarding Hong Kong. The ACP requires resources from both parties and its impact will be carried out through the next century. The Chinese and British governments are two important stakeholders in this project. Students can research the literature and identify additional stakeholders.

Can We Talk?: Communications Management for the Waste Isolation Pilot Plant, a Complex Nuclear Waste Management Project

Steven A. Goldstein, Sandia National Laboratories
Gwen M. Pullen, Sandia National Laboratories
Daniel R. Brewer, Sandia National Laboratories

PMI *Proceedings*, 1995, pp. 572–81

Synopsis

This case describes the efforts made in the United States to create a permanent radioactive waste repository located underneath the earth's surface. The project has an estimated operational life approaching fifty years and a total project cost approaching $9 billion. The case focuses on communications involved in the project, and how different communications challenges are addressed. Many challenges are faced given the contentious nature of the project. The methods describe the use of a questionnaire to develop an understanding of the public knowledge of the project and its associated technology. This case serves as an excellent example of the challenges and methods for project communications management and includes specific references to the *PMBOK Guide* section on project communications management.

Learning Objectives

Through the reading of this case and its study using the discussion questions, students should gain a better understanding of:
- project communications management
- public relations as it relates to project management
- project stakeholder management
- the challenges of managing mega-projects.

Discussion Questions and Possible Answers

1. Based on your project management knowledge, what would be an organized way of dealing with the different groups that have vested interests in the project?
    a. This case describes a project management technique which appears to use stakeholder management concerning planning, organizing, directing,

motivating, and controlling (see Cleland's *Project Management: Strategic Design and Implementation,* 2nd ed., Chapter 6, Project Stakeholder Management). This is a very effective way of managing groups with vested interests. This is also briefly described in section 2.2, The Project Management Context, of the *PMBOK Guide.*

2. The management of this case relies on the use of advanced techniques such as electronic networking, performance assessment, and a system prioritizing method. Describe one of these subprojects and comment on the feasibility of this project without the use of this tool.

   a. Electronic networking allowed for communication facilitation through E-mail and online documentation. Without the use of these techniques, the project would run into redundant and inefficient communications such as duplicate messages to project managers.

   b. Performance assessment allowed for an assessment of the project and its compliance to regulations governing its operations. The techniques used involved data collection, database creation, and simulation of possible scenarios. These techniques and the use of their technology allow for an understanding of the degree of compliance of the repository to regulations.

   c. System prioritizing is a decision-aiding analysis tool useful for balancing project constraints. It defines which activities can be combined in a viable manner. Again, its technique and technology allow the project team members to gain an understanding of the nuclear waste repository project.

3. Do you see any potential problems with the electronic networking system as it is described? What rules should be followed for the use of such a system?

   a. As it is described, there is not clear accountability for any changes made to online documents. This creates the potential for communication problems. All relevant project team members must be told in a timely manner of any changes made in the project scheduling, resource utilization, etc. A rule for using such a system is described in *PMBOK Guide,* section 10.1.1, which states that project resources should be expended only on communicating information which contributes to success or when lack of communication can lead to failure.

4. The challenge described in explaining the behavior of the waste repository describes methods and models used but ends with a statement that the full explanation of the process is impossible except to those highly technically oriented. How should this communications problem be handled? Support your answer with reference to the project management literature.

   a. The project team, through the development of the CD-ROM and survey are attempting to address the questions of those not technically oriented enough to understand the full repository technology. This planning and communications must permeate all segments of the project through communications management as described in *PMBOK Guide,* chapter 10, Project Communications Management.

5. In a project of this sort the two main challenges appear to be the use of new technology and the selling of this idea to the public. Would these two segments of the project be better handled as two distinct projects?

   a. The separation of these two segments would have both advantages and disadvantages. A disadvantage would be the perceived credibility gap in that those who understand and work with the technology would not necessarily be the spokespeople to the public. Likewise, an advantage would be the project team members responsible for the technology would not be distracted with the public relations problems.

ADDITIONAL DISCUSSION POINTS:

One of the surveys done for this project tried to determine how the general public perceived the concept of experts as unbiased depending on the source of their funding. It is an important consideration when discussing project communications to focus on what are real and perceived risks associated with a project. Students can research this real versus perceived risk topic and discuss how to handle the gap from a project management perspective.

This topic is discussed by Cleland in *Project Management: Strategic Design and Implementation*, 2nd ed., in Chapter 7 in the section on public perception and advocacy. An example of the ranking of common risks by various pubic groups is displayed in table 7.1 and the management of this problem is discussed.

The Demise of the Superconducting Supercollider: Strong Politics or Weak Management?

E. Payson Willard, PMP, Willard & Associates, Incorporated

PMI Canada *Proceedings*, 1994, pp. 1–7

Synopsis

This case explores the possible causes of the suspension of the U.S. $10 billion Department of Energy (DOE) project involved with the superconducting supercollider (SSC) in October 1993. Over $2 billion (United States' dollars) was spent on the project. During the five years that the SSC was under construction, no insurmountable technical barriers surfaced. Also a highly publicized government audit in the summer of 1993 showed the project to be basically on schedule and within budget. The case does not contain technical information and analyses of all of the stakeholders involved in the project.

Learning Objectives

This case offers the students the opportunity to analyze a failed project and to consider the reasons for its demise. It also helps in the understanding of how politics can affect a project. From the case and the questions listed, the students should gain a better understanding of:
- the mixture of science and management
- the power of stakeholders
- the importance of public relations
- project failure/project success
- mega-projects.

Discussion Questions and Possible Answers

1. The superconducting supercollider (SSC) project did not deliver what was intended. A successful project is one that not only fulfills the constraints of time, cost, and technical performance but fulfills other requirements such as minimal scope change and customer acceptance. Research in Kerzner, *Project Management: A Systems Approach to Planning, Scheduling, and Controlling*, the definition of a project success and identify which factors were not achieved in the SSC endeavor.

   a. On page 6, Kerzner shows that a successful project is one that is completed:
      1. within the allocated time period,
      2. within the cost budget,

3. at the specified performance level,
4. with acceptance by the customer/user,
5. with minimum or mutually agreed upon scope changes,
6. without disturbing the primary work of the organization, and
7. without altering the corporate culture.

The project was terminated before its completion. At the time of termination, the project had not followed the cost and schedule control system required. It was incapable, as structured, to properly control the project. However, the Department of Energy (DOE) auditors found the project to be "on schedule and within budget." Thus, it can be said that the project did conform to requirements 1–3 on the list, but did not satisfy 4–7 completely, and thus was not able to be a success. For example:

Requirement 4: The project did not have a clear customer/user and the agencies funding it were not perceived as the customer.

Requirement 5: The case clearly states that the scope was never clear and was changed several times over the life of the project.

Requirement 6: There was a poor relationship with the DOE.

Requirement 7: The special status assigned to the project differed from the typical project framework used by the DOE.

2. Why did this project fail? Was the project's failure inevitable? If not, what could have prevented the failure of the SSC?
   a. This project failed because it did not follow the five key elements of management (motivating, organizing, planning, directing, and controlling), something which probably could have been avoided. If the project's management had achieved a proper hold of the project and, for example, made the scope and objectives of the project clear, set public relations as a priority in the management of the project, and created and used the cost schedule control system and thus pleased their customers, the probability of the success of the project would have greatly increased.

3. The case exposes many factors and reasons for the SSC failure. Which do you think were the real causes and problems not properly addressed by project management?
   a. The project did not handle public relations adequately. Since its funding depended on Congress and was administrated through the DOE, they should have been recognized as important customers/stakeholders.
   b. Management never recognized the possibility that its funding could be cut.
   c. There was not a good balance between the importance of the technical and managerial groups in the project.
   d. There was a lack of scope in the project, in that the objective of the project was not clear and it was not clear what was and what was not a part of the project.

4. If Congress had voted to continue funding on the SSC, what would you have recommended as mandatory changes required to receive this funding?
   a. New experienced management, perhaps from a similar industry such as pharmaceutical or construction, with the power to affect change.
   b. The requirement of using the cost scheduling and control system, despite the adherence to the budget and schedule thus far.
   c. Clear and constant communications with the DOE and Congress, the stakeholders who control the purse strings of the project.

d. Agree on a clear scope of the project and thus minimize changes in the life of the project.
5. Public relations were mismanaged with this project. Is this the fault of the project's management? How could the project have handled the public relations, given the uncertainty of the uses of the SSC?
   a. Public relations are the responsibility of the project management and their importance should be recognized. Positives relating to the project could have been accentuated, such as the boost the SSC provided to the Texas economy and scientific world's knowledge, the jobs it provided, and commercial applications of the scientific findings.
6. Managing a project of this size requires the use of all areas of project management in order to guarantee the desired outcome. If you were in charge of a large project, on which of the nine identified processes of project management, *PMBOK Guide*, section 1.3.2, The Project Management Knowledge Areas, would you concentrate?
   a. Given the generality of the question, covering project management as a whole, all of the areas are equally important. None can be disregarded.

ADDITIONAL DISCUSSION POINTS:

In all projects there is the possibility of failure. The students should research the topic of project failures. The students can then present a failed project and discuss the key issues of that project's failure.

A good reference is *What Made Gertie Gallop: Learning from Project Failures*, O. P. Kharbanda and Jeffrey Pinto.

Boeing Spares Distribution Center: A World-Class Facility Achieved through Partnering

John R. McMichael, Lockwood Greene

PM Network, September 1994, pp. 9–19

Synopsis

This case describes the design and construction of the Boeing Spares Distribution Center at Sea Tac, Washington. This project helped to achieve rapid customer support—a key element of Boeing's relationship with its clients. The case presents the project scope, time, quality, cost, contract, procurement, communication, and risk management. The author also describes the creation of a team culture and stresses its contribution to the project's success.

Learning Objectives

This case will help the students to comprehend the following issues:
- the role of change in today's organizations
- key elements for successful projects
- the broad areas of project management applicability
- scheduling methods.

Discussion Questions and Possible Answers

1. Boeing's new Spares Distribution Center (SDC) project was very successful. From the case and your experience what are the key elements that contributed to the project's success?

    a. A number of factors contributed to the success of this project—many of which are listed directly in the case. Some of the more important elements include effective stakeholder management, good teamwork, and good communications.

    b. W. A. Randolph and B.Z. Pasner (1988), What Every Manager Needs to Know about Project Manager, *Sloan Management Review* Vol. 28, pp. 65–73, as referenced in O. Kharbanda and J. Pinto, *Successful Project Managers: Leading Your Team to Success,* Chapter 6, A Generalist, Not a Specialist, present ten elements that project managers should follow in order to increase the probability of a project's success: set a clear goal; determine the project objectives; establish checkpoints, activities, relationships, and time estimates; draw a picture of the project schedule; direct people individually and as a project team; reinforce the commitment and excitement of the project team; keep everyone connected with the project informed; build agreements that vitalize team members; empower yourself and others on the project team; and encourage risk taking and creativity.

2. The case states: "As early as 1985, the Spares organization recognized that to be responsive to the changing demands of their customers, they would have to change the way they were doing business." Change is inherent to today's organizations and business environment. Discuss some of the major changes that companies are facing today.

   a. In answering this question, the discussion might focus on the increased involvement of customers in determining project and product requirements, increasing use of automation and new technologies, and increasing competition in world markets.

   b. B.T. Barkeley and J.H. Saylor in *Customer-Driven Project Management*, Chapter 1, Introduction to Customer-Driven Project Management, present the changes organizations have to undergo to be successful in today's global environment, among others:

From:	To:
If it is not broken, do not fix it.	Continuous improvement
Functional orientation	Systems view
Inspection of defects	Prevention of defects
Accept current processes	Reengineer processes
Development	Innovation
Many rigid organizational levels	Few levels and flexible structures
Compete	Cooperate

3. The management of this project used a very effective method to deal with arising conflicts in the project. Describe the method.

   a. When conflicts were identified, they were promptly addressed and mutually beneficial solutions were developed. Solutions were evaluated according to their compliance with the mission and objectives of the project.

4. This case discusses the use of "partnering" to manage relationships with customers. Describe what is meant by partnering and discuss its benefits.

   a. The basis for partnering is found in the sidebar, "Five Manageable Truths: A Path to Partnering," in the case. The purpose of partnering is to promote better relationships between buyers and sellers. Partnering also increases flexibility, provides additional value to customers, and creates long-term relationships.

5. The schedule on this project was managed using the critical path method (CPM). Define CPM and discuss its strengths and weaknesses.

   a. The book, *Comprehensive Project Management*, Chapter 4, Project Scheduling, contains a description of the method.

   b. The *PMBOK Guide* glossary defines CPM as: "A network analysis technique used to predict project duration by analyzing which sequence of activities (which path) has the least amount of scheduling flexibility (the least amount of float). Early dates are calculated by means of a forward pass using a specific start date. Late dates are calculated by means of a backward pass starting from a specified competition date (usually the forward pass's calculated project early finish date)."

ADDITIONAL DISCUSSION POINTS:

The instructor might ask students to locate a reference to an unsuccessful large project similar to this one and draw comparisons between the management of the two projects.

Responding to the Northridge Earthquake

Jerry B. Baxter, California Department of Transportation

PM Network, November 1994, pp. 13–22

SYNOPSIS

The author describes the highways rebuilding process and transportation contingency solutions to the Northridge Earthquake in the Los Angeles area. This endeavor based its success on the California Department of Transportation single-minded determination, along with some sound project management. The case presents detailed information of the rebuilding challenge and the steps followed to achieve its goals, as well as creative solutions to the barriers found in the way.

LEARNING OBJECTIVES

This natural disaster case offers the students an unique opportunity to learn about:
- project risk management
- conflicts in projects
- innovative use of project management
- the power of incentives and disincentives.

DISCUSSION QUESTIONS AND POSSIBLE ANSWERS

1. Natural disasters happen unexpectedly and cannot be scheduled. However, the reaction to a potential misfortune can be planned and managed. Describe a method to manage these risks.

    a. The process is presented in *PMBOK Guide*, Chapter 11, Project Risk Management; the elements to consider are: risk identification, risk quantification, risk response development, and risk response control. Students should describe the activities involved in each of these steps.

2. The case states: "It was this single-minded determination, along with some sound project management, that resulted in freeways being rebuilt in a fraction of the time originally predicted, with high quality and at a reasonable price." What are the other reasons listed in the case that contributed to the success of the project?

a. The following are some of the elements mentioned in the case that influenced the success of the project:
- emergency response, management strategy, and longer-term rebuilding efforts
- fast identification of detours and alternative routes
- communication systems that identify accessibility to motorists
- economic pressure
- creativity in the solutions
- incentive/disincentive scheme
- informal bidding process
- cooperation between governmental agencies, and available procedures to gain their support if they were reluctant.

3. The challenges faced in this project included the conflicts between some agencies. Conflicts are inherent to projects—what is meant by "conflict" in a project and what are the possible courses of action that a project manager can undertake to deal with them?

   a. In *Successful Project Managers: Leading Your Team to Success*, Chapter 13, Project Management and Conflict, O. Kharbanda and J. Pinto define conflict as "the process that begins when one party perceives that one or more others have frustrated or are about to frustrate a major concern of theirs." The authors classified the possible resolution methods into three groups:
   - *Avoidance:* The project manager is neutral, the parties work out their concerns on their own.
   - *Defusion:* The project manager helps by letting time pass until the problem has cooled down and the parties can work out their differences in a rational way.
   - *Confrontation:* The project manager tries to determine the cause of the conflict and resolve it with the parties involved.

4. All organizations should have a crisis management plan in place to deal with unexpected disasters. From the literature or your own experience describe a situation when an organization was successfully or unsuccessfully able to deal with a crisis. What led to the success or failure?

   a. Some possible situations include the Tylenol poisonings, syringes discovered in cans of Pepsi, U.S. Air's response to plane crashes, the Challenger disaster, etc.

ADDITIONAL DISCUSSION POINTS:

This project had to be executed at an accelerated pace. Unfortunately, quality is often one of the elements that is sacrificed in situations such as this. The students can work in groups and develop tactics to guarantee that none of the key elements of a project are disregarded because of schedule constraints. The *PMBOK Guide* offers some advice on how to handle quality and accelerated schedules in Section 8, Project Quality Management, and Section 5, Project Scope Management.

A Town Makes History by Rising to New Heights

Bruce Watson

Smithsonian, June 1996, pp. 110–20

Synopsis

This case describes the challenges faced by Valmeyer, an Illinois town. In July 1993, Valmeyer was hit by a flood; after the disaster some of its residents, with help from the Federal Emergency Management Administration (FEMA) and the involvement of twenty-two finance and construction government agencies, built a new town in a nearby flood safe area. This project that initially was planned to take seven years took little longer than two years, thanks to a visionary leader and the strength of the residents. The case depicts some of the building processes and concentrates on its human and management challenges.

Learning Objectives

This case will provide the student with a general sense of the wide applicability of project management. From the discussion of the case, the students will gain a better comprehension of the following issues in a project:
- the leader's role
- the different reactions to the same disaster or shortcoming
- the power of vision
- people's versatility.

Discussion Questions and Possible Answers

1. Throughout the building of the new town, the mayor was the person who quietly held the town of Valmeyer together. He was the project leader even though there was not a formal project or a project manager. What are the characteristics of a project leader?

   a. The *PMBOK Guide*, Section 2.4.1, Leading, states that leaders are the ones who give direction to the organization (vision), align people (build consensus needed to achieve the vision), and motivate and inspire people in order to energize them into overcoming the obstacles and barriers to change.

   b. Leaders establish a "vision" or purpose and "do the right thing." The instructor may wish to discuss examples of other successful leaders (who were not necessarily managers).

   c. Other characteristics include personal ambition; ability to listen, debate, and gather facts; ability to balance tasks; ability to make and execute decisions; ability to see the best in people and motivate performance; ability to be a mentor; an understanding of the technology involved in a particular project; intelligence; ability to delegate and let go of control, etc.

2. VISIONS—Valmeyer Integrating Sustainably into Our New Setting—besides being a creative acronym, was also the vision of the leader who helped to build the new town. Define the concept of vision and its importance in the project management context.

   a. B.T. Barkeley and J.H. Saylor in *Customer-Driven Project Management*, Chapter 3, Customer-Driven Project Management: An Integrated Approach, define vision as: "The future image of the organization, the scenario of where the organization leadership wants to go ...Vision is articulated first by top management, and then it is worked through the organization by means on 'focus' teams. Vision is the outlook of the organization to be prospering long into the future."

3. The case presents the feelings of the people affected by the flood, and some of the problems they had with neighboring towns. The author specifically discusses the situation Anna Glaenzer ran into at a local store, when buying some jeans. What could be done in order to reduce this kind of friction?

   a. An appropriate approach would be to identify the stakeholders of the project in the nearby communities and effectively communicate the situations of new Valmeyer residents. The key elements of this process are described in *PMBOK Guide*, Section 10, Project Communication Management.

4. The case illustrates how people got involved in the different teams building the new town and how they handled those new challenges. Discuss these efforts from a project perspective of managing time, cost, and technical performance objectives.

   a. From a cost perspective the townspeople had to be concerned with working within budget that were preset by insurance and governmental agencies. Although the teams may not have had specific time deadlines, certainly there was a concern about quickly building new homes. Project management scheduling techniques could have been used to estimate times and establish deadlines. This may have shortened the time that families had to wait for new homes. Technical performance objectives were not formally established for the town but also may have been better controlled using a project management approach.

ADDITIONAL DISCUSSION POINTS:

The instructor might ask each student to describe a leader with which he is familiar (historically known or from a personal experience). The students can present the characteristics (as discussed in question 1) that made the leader successful or unsuccessful.

Real-World Challenges to a Multinational Project Team: Building a Manufacturing Facility in India

Edward A. O'Connor, Bausch & Lomb, Inc.

PMI Canada *Proceedings*, 1994, pp. 377–80

SYNOPSIS

Bausch & Lomb invested in a $13 million joint venture in India to produce and market high quality eye care and optical products in India and adjacent countries. The project concentrated initially on the support and development of the soft contact lenses business. The author describes some project challenges that are common to developing countries, such as: complex governmental procedures, low manufacturing expertise, cultural differences, and distinct management practices. The case depicts the scope, time, quality, risk, and communication management of the project. The endeavor was completed under budget and meeting all the deliverables for product cost and quality.

LEARNING OBJECTIVES

From this international case and through its discussion, the students will gain a further comprehension of:
- project's critical success factors
- team work, team members
- project management ethics
- project quality management.

DISCUSSION QUESTIONS AND POSSIBLE ANSWERS

1. The author stresses the importance of designing and building the facility to produce products and systems in accordance with international quality standards. Project quality management is a key element in the success of any project. Define project quality management and the processes involved in it.
    a. *PMBOK Guide,* Section 8, Project Quality Management, states: "Project Quality Management includes the processes required to ensure that the project will satisfy the needs for which it was undertaken. It includes 'all activities of the overall management function that determine the quality policy, objectives, and responsibilities and implements them by means such as quality planning, quality control, quality assurance, and quality improvement, within the quality system.'" —From another

source: The International Organization for Standardization. 1993. Quality—Vocabulary (Draft International Standard 8402). Geneva, Switzerland: ISO Press—the major processes are:
- "Quality Planning—identifying which quality standards are relevant to the project and determine how to satisfy them.
- Quality Assurance—evaluating overall project performance on a regular basis to provide confidence that the project will satisfy the relevant quality standards.
- Quality Control—monitoring specific project results to determine if they comply with relevant quality standards and identify ways to eliminate causes of unsatisfactory performance."

2. The case states: "Team members were selected by the project manager for their expertise, their flexibility toward foreign cultures and their ability to work as part of a multinational team." Under what circumstances might a team member be removed from the project?

   a. H. Kerzner, in *Project Management: A Systems Approach to Planning, Scheduling, and Controlling*, Chapter 4, Organizing and Staffing the Project Office and Team, suggests that employees must be removed from the project due to:
   - disobedience of rules, orders, policies, and procedures
   - disregard of the established formal authority
   - personal agenda above company loyalty
   - non acceptance of a trade between technical, budget, and schedule issues
   - incompetence.

3. The author notes that Bausch & Lomb's style of management was quite different from the typical style in Indian firms. Discuss the importance of recognizing and managing cultural differences on large projects.

   a. Culture is a set of behaviors, beliefs, and customers that determine a society's "way of life." An organization also has a culture with it's own set of preferred behaviors. The organization's culture will be framed by the country's cultural preferences. For example, in many foreign nations women are not yet accepted in the work force and therefore may not be accepted as members of a project team. Bausch & Lomb's participative style contradicted the typical autocratic style that was characteristic of most Indian firms. This required Bausch & Lomb to carefully select project team members to be certain that they were flexible in dealing with foreign cultures. Project managers must be careful to consider how certain behaviors and management preferences might be viewed by foreign stakeholders. A training course that focuses on the culture of the foreign country in which the project is to operate may be appropriate for the project team.

   b. If international students are present in the classroom, the instructor might asked them to highlight differences between the United States' culture and their own.

4. The author notes that a number of external risks were unpredictable. These became important strategic issues for the project. Define and discuss a process for managing "strategic issues."

   a. Strategic issues can be any factor or force that can significantly affect an organization's future strategies and tactics. Project owners must be aware of the possible and probable impacts of strategic issues, and project managers must focus project resources on dealing with them. Strategic issues can be cultural, political, environmental, social, financial/economic, organizational, legal, technological, or competitive. How should strategic issues be managed?

    b. Four key steps are important to managing strategic issues: issue identification, issue assessment (judging the importance of an issue in terms of its impact on the project), identification of action, and implementation of actions. (Adapted from Cleland, David I., *Project Management: Strategic Design and Implementation*, 2nd ed., Chapter 7, Strategic Issues in Project Management.)

5. Project managers are sometimes challenged with major bureaucratic obstacles in an endeavor. This fact can generate ethical dilemmas for the project manager (i.e., looking for short-cuts). Read PMI's Code of Ethics for the Project Management Profession (see Appendix A) and discuss its impact on your own work.

    a. In addition to other points, the Code of Ethics for the Project Management Profession (see Appendix A) states: "Project Management professionals shall maintain high standards of personal and professional conduct and obey the laws of the country in which work is being performed." Students should give examples of how this and some of the other requirements play a role in the decisions that they make.

ADDITIONAL DISCUSSION POINTS:

Students should select a project management situation from their work or school experience. They should then identify three or four key strategic issues for that situation, assess the impact of the issues on the project, and list possible actions for dealing with them. This can be a completed project, an ongoing project, or an upcoming project. Remind students to identify stakeholders as they identify the strategic issues.

Total Quality Management and Project Management

D.H. Stamatis, Contemporary Consultants

Project Management Journal, September 1994, pp. 48–54

Synopsis

This case describes the use of project management principles as an excellent tool for implementing total quality management (TQM) in any organization. The author stresses the fact that TQM is people dependent and relies on the use of cross-functional teams. The paper also presents guidelines on how to implement TQM through projects management and discusses how project management and TQM fit.

Learning Objectives

Through the discussion of this case, students should gain a better understanding of:
- teams
- the matrix organization
- the relation between planning and implementing
- the wide applicability of project management.

Discussion Questions and Possible Answers

1. The author recommends the implementation of TQM through project management (i.e., TQM implementation is considered a "project"). What are the key elements that define a project?
    a. The case uses reference 5 (Kerzner) to define a project: "A project, on the other hand, is an undertaking that has a beginning, an end, and is carried out to meet established goals within specific costs, schedules, quality objectives."
    b. The *PMBOK Guide* glossary defines a project: "A temporary endeavor undertaken to create a unique product or service."
    c. Cleland, in *Project Management: Strategic Design and Implementation*, 2nd ed., p. 4, states: "A project consists of a combination of organizational resources pulled together to create something that did not previously exist and that will provide a performance capability in the design and execution of organizational strategies."

2. What is the difference between a project and a program? Is TQM a project or a program?
   a. A program is an ongoing resource-consuming endeavor that has a specific purpose, for example, a productivity improvement program, a corporate suggestion program, a new hire training program, etc. Programs are often composed of different projects. In a productivity program several projects could be involved such as machine tool modernization, employee training, or reengineering projects.
   b. Some might say TQM is a program; some, a project; still others may say it is neither. The case really focuses on TQM implementation as a project. TQM is actually a set of management philosophies and practices that may include both specific projects and programs.
3. The author states that the matrix structure is part of the transformation of the organization toward TQM. What are the shortcomings of the matrix organization?
   a. H. Kerzner, in *Project Management: A Systems Approach to Planning, Scheduling, and Controlling*, Chapter 3, Organizational Structures, as paraphrased, among others identifies the following disadvantages: multidimensional information and work flow, dual reporting, changing priorities, opposing management and project goals, potential for conflict, difficult monitoring and controlling, biased functional managers, and difficult to manage functional/project organization balance of power and role ambiguity.
4. Teams are inherent to any TQM endeavor. What are the features that differentiate teams from just groups of people?
   a. From the case: "They produce high-quality and high-value products and services. They perform well against known internal and external standards. They use significantly fewer resources than one would expect. They generate a sense of enthusiasm and excitement among their members and those who come in contact with them."
   b. From Bursic, Karen M., Self-Managed Production (Manufacturing) Teams in Cleland, David I. *Field Guide to Project Management*.
      - Teams typically consist of anywhere from five to fifteen members with different skills and knowledge.
      - Teams are a formal, recognized part of the organization and create a departure from traditional organizational designs.
      - Teams are intentionally established with a common purpose and particular tasks.
      - Team members participate in regular meetings for various purposes.
      - Teams allow for shared authority, responsibility, and accountability for decisions and results through participation and involvement.
      - Teams participate in activities such as team-building sessions, problem solving training, implementation of team decisions, and presentations of results to management. During these activities workers are specifically referred to and defined as teams.
5. What project management tools and techniques can be applied to the implementation of TQM?
   a. Answers to this question are many but might include the use of scheduling techniques such as PERT and CPM, the use of a cost management

system, establishment of a project manager and team, scope management to define the project boundaries, and so forth.

ADDITIONAL DISCUSSION POINTS:

The author stresses the importance of the implementation phase of the project and states: "The lesson may be that a complete formula without method for company-wide implementation will not guarantee the desired final product." In small groups, the students should discuss the importance of the implementation stage and its relationship with the planning phase.

PMBOK Guide, Section 3.3, Process Interactions, gives a general framework of the relationship between the design and implementation phase.

Organization and Management of a Multi-Organizational Single Responsibility Project

The James H. Campbell Power Plant Unit #3

M. P. Shrontz, Project Manager, Consumers Power Company
G. M. Porter, Vice President and Project Manager, Townsend and Bottum, Inc.
N. L. Scott, Senior Projects Manager, Gilbert/Commonwealth

PMI *Proceedings*, 1977, pp. 258–64.

Synopsis

This case describes the organization and management of Consumers Power Company's James H. Campbell Plant Unit #3 project. The authors discuss the use of a single responsibility contract and its effect on the overall project management process. The case also describes the use of team-building sessions for identifying problems and using team action to solve them. Various aspects of quality and productivity improvement efforts are also discussed.

Learning Objectives

Although this case is very broad in nature and discusses many aspects of project management, it focuses on a number of topics of quality management. These include the placement of the quality function within the overall project structure, the team-building sessions used to improve the quality of the team process, and the quality assurance program. Objectives include:
- discussion of where to place the quality assurance function within the project organization structure
- focus on the team-building sessions used on the Campbell Plant project and the benefits of these sessions with respect to the quality of the team process and management of project interfaces
- understand the quality assurance program described in the case and discuss its benefits and drawbacks.

Discussion Questions and Possible Answers

1. What are the characteristics of an effective team? Do you think these characteristics are present in less effective groups?
    a. O. Kharbanda and J. Pinto in *Successful Project Managers: Leading Your Team to Success*, Chapter 12, Team Building, as paraphrased, state that

the qualities that effective teams normally have are missing in less effective groups. The factors that are most often listed as characteristics of successful teams include:
- *Clear sense of mission:* The sense of mission must be collectively accepted by all team members and clearly understood.
- *Understanding the team's interdependencies:* Team members have to know their contribution to the project and how their work fits into the overall endeavor.
- *Cohesiveness:* How much attraction there is among team members and their tasks.
- *Trust:* It is manifested in the belief among team members that they are able to disagree without concern about retaliation.
- *Enthusiasm:* The belief among team members if the goal is achievable and the positive energy associated.

  b. Other characteristics of successful teams include: senior management support, interdisciplinary and diverse membership, integration into the organizational design, education and training, effective leadership, effective facilitation, clear team mission, objectives and goals, strong team chartering process, clear team roles and responsibilities, and a balance of authority, responsibility, and accountability (paraphrased from Bursic, Karen M., Self-Managed Production (Manufacturing) Teams, in Cleland, David I., editor, *Field Guide to Project Management*.

2. How can funds allocation and top management support be solicited for team-building programs?

   a. First, it is vitally important for supporters to demonstrate the importance of the team concept to top management. The project manager should emphasize the ability to increase performance through the use of project team building and development. Cases that support the use of team building can be presented in order to justify expenditures.

3. Demonstrate your understanding of the quality assurance program described in the case. What are some of the benefits and drawbacks of the program?

   a. Students should be able to understand the purpose of the program and how it is used to establish reliability levels for the various project systems. Benefits might include increased communication to project team members with regard to the quality requirements of various systems while drawbacks might include the increase in paper work and time devoted to the process.

4. The teams formed out of the building sessions are interdisciplinary teams made up of members from design engineers, construction engineers, schedulers, estimators, purchasers, and inspectors. Due to the development of such a team, many positive effects are felt in the project. This type of team is also known as a product-process team or the concurrent engineering process. What are the advantages to this type of team or process?

   a. In *Project Management: Strategic Design and Implementation*, 2nd ed., by Cleland, p. 64, the following advantages of concurrent engineering teams, as paraphrased, are listed:
   1. Close interaction between engineering, marketing, and manufacturing.
   2. An increase in the possibility of success of the endeavor.

3. Products/services get to the market sooner.
4. Organizational resources are used more effectively and efficiently.
5. People working in these teams have a higher degree of ownership of the product or process being developed.
6. Due to the different backgrounds and disciplines of the members of the team, the checks and balances are checked for a wider range of considerations.
7. Time is saved. Time represents money and profits when the product or service is introduced into the market.

Other information on this subject is included in Chapter 10 of *The Strategic Management Of Teams* by Cleland, p. 198.

ADDITIONAL DISCUSSION POINTS:

The instructor might wish to discuss other kinds of quality assurance programs and their benefits as well as the justification of expenditures for such programs. Students might also give examples of such programs from their own work experiences.

Prudent and Reasonable Project Management

David I. Cleland, University of Pittsburgh

Project Management Journal, December 1985, pp. 90–97

Synopsis

The purpose of this case is to present a general model for determining what constitutes "prudent and reasonable" project management. This model, referred to as the project management system (PMS), is comprised of six interrelated subsystems, each having a specific purpose. Using the PMS as a basis, the overall management of the Trans-Alaskan Pipeline System (TAPS) project and the resulting problems are evaluated based on the definitions of reasonable and prudent. In the 1980s, the state of Alaska alleged before the federal Energy Regulatory Commission and the Alaska Public Utilities Commission that $1.6 billion in imprudent management costs were associated with the design, engineering, and construction of the $8 billion Trans-Alaska Pipeline System. The TAPS project experience clearly points out the need to adequately address all of the various aspects and subsystems of project management.

Learning Objectives

Through the use of the project management system model, the students will understand what constitutes prudent and reasonable management of a project. In addition, the student should be exposed to the six interrelated areas or subsystems that need to be properly utilized in order to minimize the risk of cost overruns and schedule delays. When discussing this case, the following points should be addressed:
- some of the characteristics of prudent and reasonable project management
- the relationship between prudent and reasonable management practices and risk management
- the components of the project management system and their importance
- the impact of ignoring some of the project management aspects or PMS components.

Discussion Questions and Possible Answers

1. What constitutes reasonable and prudent management? What are some specific traits of a prudent and reasonably managed project?
   a. Prudent and reasonable management emphasizes the need to effectively and efficiently allocate resources so as to ensure the successful attainment of the project's objectives and goals. Specifically, this concept

correctly means applying the most appropriate project management techniques and methods available to ensure that a project is completed on time, within budget, and in conformance with the desired performance requirements. The students may also provide a definition that conveys the various legal responsibilities of the project owner and contractor. The prudent and reasonable management of projects encompasses the following key areas:
- the project owner or sponsor taking the initiative to establish an organization that will provide and support effective strategic planning and management
- devising a project management system to serve as a model for organizational strategy while also instilling a special type of management philosophy
- the practicing of proven, modern project management techniques in the execution of the key management functions: planning, organizing, motivating, leading, and controlling.

2. As a project manager what methods can be used to identify risks?

   a. *PMBOK Guide*, Section 11.1.2, Tools and Techniques for Risk Identification, identifies the following methods:

   Checklist: Checklists are typically organized by source of risk. Sources include the project context, other process outputs, the product of the project technology issues, and internal sources such as team member skills (or the lack of them). Some applications areas have widely used classification schemes for sources of risk.

   Flowcharting: Flowcharting can help the project team better understand the causes and effects of risks.

   Interviewing: Risk-oriented interviews with various stakeholders may help identify risk not identified during normal planning activities. Records of pre-project interviews may also be available.

3. How does prudent and reasonable management relate to risk management?

   a. Both types of management have the same goals of effectively and efficiently using resources to successfully complete the project on time and within budget. In order for a project to be handled in a truly prudent and reasonable fashion, all associated risks and uncertainties must be considered. Some of these risks may have to be further managed or accounted for in the project plans, depending on their impact and likelihood. Both are dependent on the successful use and application of appropriate project management techniques. In order to reduce a project's risk, each one of the project management subsystems needs to be fully addressed and properly utilized.

4. What is the project management system? Briefly describe each of the six subsystems.

   a. A project management system (PMS) is a set of six interrelated subsystems that each perform a particular function which contributes to the total project management system.

   Organizational Subsystem: The organizational subsystem provides the foundation for the management of projects characterized by an organizational design with appropriate authority, responsibility, and accountability relationships.

Planning Subsystem: The planning subsystem deals with the selection of project objectives and goals as well as the strategies for the use of resources to accomplish project ends. These strategies include plans of action, policies, procedures, resource allocation schemes, and the productive use of organizational resources.

Control Subsystem: The project control subsystem establishes performance standards for the project schedule, budget, and technical performance objectives and then compares the actual progress to these standards. Another primary function of the system is to alert the project team to any potential problems so that corrective action can be taken.

Management Information Subsystem: The management information subsystem contains the intelligence or processed data that is needed to effectively plan and control the project. This information enables the key managers to track the consumption of resources and the actual project results obtained.

Cultural Subsystem: The cultural ambiance of a project is simply a collection of ideas and beliefs that are shared by managers and the project team members and serve to form the basis for the existing organizational culture. The culture that is developed becomes a unique characteristic of the organization and in turn has an influence on many other aspects of the organization.

Human Subsystem: The human subsystem emphasizes the important role played by various individuals. In short, the outcome of a project is ultimately dependent on the combined performance of its team members along with individuals and managers who provide functional support.

5. Considering each one of these subsystems, describe any problems resulting from the management of the Trans-Alaska Pipeline System (TAPS). In your discussion, be sure to point out any overlooked project risks.

   a. Organizational Subsystem:
      I. The TAPS Ownership Committee did not specifically define its strategic role nor was anyone else given that responsibility. As a result, several key strategic issues were left to chance. In particular, TAPS did not resolve key strategic issues that included: (1) developing a master project plan; (2) early integrated life-cycle project planning; (3) developing an organizational design strategy for Alyeska, the owners, and the construction management contractor; (4) design and implementation of a comprehensive project management information system; (5) developing an effective control system for the project; and (6) the confusion of responsibilities between Alyeska and Bechtel which resulted in an overlap and duplication of functions.
      II. The Owners Construction Committee never developed a master project plan that could guide its organizational design for the TAPS project. Without the strategy, it could not define work packages and the roles of the various parties involved in the project. Unless authority and responsibility relationships were developed between the organizations, there is a serious danger of costly and inefficient duplication of effort as well as the risk that some of the work packages would not have anyone assigned appropriate responsibility.

III. Alyeska constituted an intervening layer of management and professionals in the hierarchy of the TAPS organization. This layering increased the distance between top level members of the committee and the front-line supervisors directly involved with accomplishing the work packages.

Planning Subsystem: The owners and Alyeska did not ensure the preparation of adequate, comprehensive plans at the owner's level. Even though PERT/CPM was a widely used project management tool, the owners failed to use it as a network planning and scheduling tool. Without proper project planning, there is little basis for making comparisons, and it becomes very difficult to identify problems. Even if the problems are detected, the lack of planning makes it virtually impossible to develop feasible alternate courses of action, such as resource realignment.

Control Subsystem: Construction was started before adequate, thorough planning had been accomplished, resulting in inadequate project control systems. Without an adequate planning and control subsystem, there was no real way to determine the progress of the project or assess project risk.

Management Information Subsystem: Inadequate information on the TAPS project contributed to the lack of meaningful and useful controls. In short, project managers cannot manage what they cannot measure, or evaluate.

Cultural Subsystem: The fundamental problem here was the aura of distrust and questionable credibility being attributed to key people in Alyeska and the major contractors.

Human Subsystem: The case also notes that Alyeska's poor labor management was a major contributor to excesses. Specifically, TAPS construction began without adequate housing, catering control, or communications facilities in place.

ADDITIONAL DISCUSSION POINTS:

Since the case primarily dealt with the prudent and reasonable management practices that were lacking on the Trans-Alaska Pipeline System project, the instructor might want to present a case that demonstrates the correct application of the project management system. Another option available is for the instructor to present some of the various project management techniques that could be used to properly establish and maintain each one of the PMS subsystems.

The use of the article, The Legal Standards for Prudent Project Management, by Randall L. Speck, PMI *Proceedings*, 1987, pp. 566–76, to promote further discussion by the students should be considered.

The Space Shuttle Challenger Incident

Edited by Francis M. Webster, Jr.

Project Management Journal, June 1987, pp. 41–68

SYNOPSIS

This case describes some of the project management problems that contributed to the flawed decision to launch the space shuttle Challenger that subsequently ended in tragedy. First, the case provides the necessary background on the space shuttle program. Next, it describes all of the key actions that eventually led to the decision to launch the shuttle on the morning of January 28, 1986. The case concludes with the findings and recommendations of the Rogers Commission on ways to improve the project management organization.

LEARNING OBJECTIVES

This case will demonstrate not only the importance of risk management, but also the need to continually emphasize the tools available to minimize risks. An organization must do more than simply go through the necessary motions. It must show commitment and support for efforts to reduce the likelihood of project failure. After discussing this case, the students should understand the following points:
- Faulty planning can often lead to taking additional and unnecessary project risks.
- Risk management must be an inherent part of the organization's planning and operating procedures.
- The management structure and operating policies can also contribute to unnecessary risk taking.
- The importance of an organizational environment that actively supports programs and/or specific efforts designed to reduce project risk.

DISCUSSION QUESTIONS AND POSSIBLE ANSWERS

1. According to the *PMBOK Guide*, what is the concept of the work breakdown structure (WBS)? Compare the planning process in this case to that of developing a work breakdown structure and describe some of the difficulties encountered when planning for the launch schedule.
    a. In the *PMBOK Guide*, section 5.3.3, Outputs From Scope Definition, a work breakdown structure is a deliverable-oriented grouping of project elements that organizes and defines the total scope of the project.
    b. The planning process took from twelve to eighteen months and involved a series of repetitive iterations that defined the flight design in increasing

detail. The process can be compared to starting with a work breakdown structure, separating it into key activities, and then further subdividing these activities until the smallest definable element, namely the work package, is obtained. In both cases, once the activities have been defined, they are scheduled according to precedent constraints so as to satisfy milestone dates. Since the planning started in 1984, ten major document changes, that added or deleted payload items, disrupted the preparation process. As a result of this rather involved process, significant changes were made that required an extensive amount of time to incorporate. In addition, the closer the changes were made to the launch date the more serious the repercussions on the overall schedule. The launch appeared to be planned without regards to some of the other missions. Specifically, delays in the 61-C mission forced further slips in the shuttle launch date. The level of resources available was not capable of adequately handling the additional workload generated by the increasing flight rate. In short, the planning process did not consider NASA's resource constraints.

2. Describe the problems existing in the shuttle program management structure and the communication process that contributed to the flawed launch decision.

   a. There was an overall failure in the communication process that resulted in a launch decision being made on insufficient and misleading information. Further compounding this problem was the NASA organizational structure that permitted internal flight safety problems to completely bypass the shuttle managers.
   b. The people who made the decision to launch were unaware of the past history of problems plaguing the O-rings and the joints. In addition, the group was never made aware of the contractors' written recommendation to avoid launching the shuttle when the temperature was below 53 degrees Fahrenheit.
   c. During the launch preparation, the concerns of the contractors and the lower-level NASA managers to whom they reported were not communicated to the senior levels of NASA management. Specifically, the commission's investigation revealed that the Marshall Space Flight Center attempted to resolve problems internally rather than passing the information on to upper management. At the urging of the Marshall Space Flight Center, the managers at the Morton Thiokol Company (the company that manufactured the solid rocket boosters) disregarded the concerns of their engineers and dropped their objections against the launch of the shuttle.

3. Explain the organizational and environmental factors that led to the overall decreased concern for safety, reliability, and quality assurance. How is this related to project risk management?

   Initially, the shuttle program was in a development phase with all of the resources being concentrated on the successful completion of a single flight. Later the program switched to an operational setting with the same resources being used on several missions simultaneously. The pressure of trying to increase the number of flights within the same resource constraints resulted in an attempt to streamline the launch process through the use of automation, standardization, and centralized management. As a result of NASA's past success and safety record, a "can do" attitude had developed at NASA that had a tendency to de-emphasize the importance of safety, quality, and reliability.

The NASA point of reference had changed so that it expected the contractor to prove that the launch was unsafe, rather than that it was safe. Due in part to budgetary constraints, the number of people working on safety, reliability, and quality assurance was reduced at the Marshall Space Center and NASA.

Another contributing factor was the way the various safety, reliability, and quality assurance units reported to the supervisors who were responsible for processing. The thrust of the safety, reliability, and quality assurance programs was to reduce the risk associated with a mission. These programs played a key part in the risk management of the shuttle program. This is partly carried out through the use of standardized procedures, checklists, and system component inspections. Considering that the shuttle must be able to perform in a hostile space environment where any small malfunction could be critical, the importance of risk management simply can not be over stressed.

4. Describe the commission's recommendations aimed at improving the overall management of the shuttle program. Do you agree with these recommendations?

   a. The recommendations were:
      - The shuttle program structure needs to be revised so that the project managers of the various elements are held more accountable to the overall shuttle program as opposed to their own management groups.
      - The program manager's responsibility needs to be increased so that the manager has authority over all space transportation systems (STS) operations. In particular, all program funding and all shuttle program work at the centers need to be clearly under the program manager's authority.
      - NASA should establish an STS safety advisory panel that reports to the STS program manager. The panel will have the overall responsibility for operational issues, launch commit criteria, flight rules, flight readiness, and risk management.
      - NASA needs to establish an office of safety, reliability, and quality assurance to be headed by an associate administrator working directly for the NASA administrator. This will create an independent office that is high enough in the organization to get the emphasis it deserves.
      - NASA must revise its flight rate so that it is consistent with its resources. In addition, policies need to be enacted that restrict changes that are made to the cargo manifesto.
      - NASA needs to establish an environment that encourages the timely flow of information without the use of censorship.

5. The National Space Transportation System (NSTS) project did not deliver what was intended. A successful project is one that not only fulfills the constraints of time, cost, and technical performance but fulfills other requirements such as minimal scope change and customer acceptance. Describe the requirements of a successful project.

General

      a. In *Project Management: A Systems Approach to Planning, Scheduling, and Controlling*, p. 6, Kerzner states that a project's success depends on the fulfillment of the endeavors:
      1. Within the allocated time period;
      2. Within the budgeted cost;
      3. At the proper performance or specification level;
      4. With acceptance by the customer/user;
      5. With minimum or mutually agreed upon scope changes;
      6. Without disturbing the main work of the organization;
      7. Without changing the corporate culture.

ADDITIONAL DISCUSSION POINTS:

The instructor may want to take the case discussion a step further and actually talk about the action taken by NASA following the commission's report. The instructor may also draw from some of the current news items on the shuttle program and use them to lead a class discussion on how well the program has done since these changes were made. In addition, the instructor could raise the question of whether or not all of the problems have actually been corrected.

The students could also analyze which of those factors identified in question 5 were not achieved in the NSTS endeavor and could be responsible for the Challenger incident.

Appendix A

CODE OF ETHICS FOR THE PROJECT MANAGEMENT PROFESSION

PREAMBLE: Project Management Professionals, in the pursuit of the profession, affect the quality of life for all people in our society. Therefore, it is vital that Project Management Professionals conduct their work in an ethical manner to earn and maintain the confidence of team members, colleagues, employees, employers, clients, and the public.

ARTICLE I: Project Management Professionals shall maintain high standards of personal and professional conduct, and:

a. Accept responsibility for their actions.

b. Undertake projects and accept responsibility only if qualified by training or experience, or after full disclosure to their employers or clients of pertinent qualifications.

c. Maintain their professional skills at the state of the art and recognize the importance of continued personal development and education.

d. Advance the integrity and prestige of the profession by practicing in a dignified manner.

e. Support this code and encourage colleagues and co-workers to act in accordance with this code.

f. Support the professional society by actively participating and encouraging colleagues and co-workers to participate.

g. Obey the laws of the country in which work is being performed.

ARTICLE II: Project Management Professionals shall, in their work:

a. Provide the necessary project leadership to promote maximum productivity while striving to minimize costs.

b. Apply state-of-the-art project management tools and techniques to ensure quality, cost, and time objectives, as set forth in the project plan, are met.

c. Treat fairly all project team members, colleagues, and co-workers, regardless of race, religion, sex, age, or national origin.

d. Protect project team members from physical and mental harm.

e. Provide suitable working conditions and opportunities for project team members.

f. Seek, accept, and offer honest criticism of work, and properly credit the contribution of others.

g. Assist project team members, colleagues, and co-workers in their professional development.

ARTICLE III: Project Management Professionals shall, in their relations with employers and clients:

a. Act as faithful agents or trustees for their employers and clients in professional and business matters.

b. Keep information on the business affairs or technical process of an employer or client in confidence while employed, and later, until such information is properly released.

c. Inform their employers, clients, professional societies, or public agencies of which they are members, or to which they may make any presentations, of any circumstance that could lead to a conflict of interest.

d. Neither give nor accept, directly or indirectly, any gift, payment, or service of more than nominal value to or from those having business relationships with their employers or clients.

e. Be honest and realistic in reporting project quality, cost, and time.

Appendix A

ARTICLE IV: Project Management Professionals shall, in fulfilling their responsibilities to the community:

a. Protect the safety, health, and welfare of the public and speak out against abuses in these areas affecting the public interest.

b. Seek to extend public knowledge and appreciation of the project management profession and its achievements.

Appendix B

RECOMMENDED READING

Badiru, Adedji B., and P. Simin Pulat. 1994. *Comprehensive Project Management: Integrating Optimization Model, Management Principles and Computers.* Prentice Hall.

Barkley, Bruce T., and James H. Saylor. 1994. *Customer-Driven Project Management.* McGraw-Hill Professional Book Group.

Cleland, David I. 1986. *Project Management: Strategic Design and Implementation.* McGraw-Hill Professional Book Group.

———. 1994. *Project Management: Strategic Design and Implementation.* 2nd ed. McGraw-Hill Professional Book Group.

———. 1996. *Strategic Management of Teams.* Van Nostrand Reinhold.

———, ed. *Field Guide to Project Management.* 1997. Van Nostrand Reinhold.

Fisher, Roger, and William Ury. 1992. *Getting to Yes: Negotiating Agreement Without Giving In.* Houghton Mifflin Co.

Kerzner, Harold. 1995. *Project Management: A Systems Approach to Planning, Scheduling and Controlling.* Van Nostrand Reinhold.

Kharbanda, O.P., and Jeffrey K. Pinto. 1996. *What Made Gertie Gallop: Learning from Project Failures.* Van Nostrand Reinhold.

King, W.R., and D.I. Cleland, eds. *Strategic Planning and Management Handbook.* 1986. Van Nostrand Reinhold.

Morris, Peter W.G. 1994. *The Management of Projects.* Thomas Telford Publications.

Pinto, Jeffrey K., and O.P. Kharbanda. 1997. *Successful Project Managers: Leading Your Team to Success.* Van Nostrand Reinhold.

PMI's Tools for Training

PROJECT MANAGEMENT CASEBOOK

Most project managers would agree that the best way to learn new concepts and techniques is to practice them as you learn them. The case study approach has proven to be an effective way to demonstrate the practical applications of project management theory, and the case studies presented in this book show you how and why projects are used in a wide variety of organizational settings in contemporary life. Fifty cases are categorized by one of following areas: planning, organizing, motivating, directing, controlling, and general.

Edited by David Cleland, Karen Bursic, Richard Puerzer, and A. Yaroslav Vlasak
ISBN: 1-880410-45-1

A GUIDE TO THE PROJECT MANAGEMENT BODY OF KNOWLEDGE™

The basic management reference for everyone who works on projects. Serves as a tool for learning about the generally accepted knowledge and practices of the profession. As "management by projects" becomes more and more a recommended business practice worldwide, the *PMBOK™ Guide* becomes an essential source of information that should be on every manager's bookshelf. Available in hardcover or paperback, the *PMBOK™ Guide* is an official standards document of the Project Management Institute.

ISBN: 1-880410-12-5 (paperback), 1-880410-13-3 (hardcover)

INTERACTIVE PMBOK™ GUIDE

This CD-ROM in multimedia format makes it easy for you to access the valuable information in PMI's *A Guide to the Project Management Body of Knowledge™*. Features hypertext links for easy reference—simply click on underlined works in the text, and the software will take you to that particular section in the *PMBOK™ Guide*. Minimum system requirements: 486 PC, 8MB RAM, 10MB free disk space, CD-ROM drive, mouse or other pointing device, and Windows 3.1 or greater.

PMBOK™ REVIEW PACKAGE

This "Box of Books" offers you a set of materials that supplements the *PMBOK™ Guide* in helping you develop a deeper understanding of the Project Management Body of Knowledge™ and helps you prepare for the PMP Certification exam. These important and authoritative publications offer the depth and breadth you need to learn more about all the *PMBOK™ Guide* knowledge areas. Includes the following titles—*Project Management: A Managerial Approach*; *Project Planning, Scheduling & Control*; *Human Resource Skills for the Project Manager*; *Project and Program Risk Management*; *Quality Management for Projects & Programs*; *PMBOK™ Q&A*; *Managing the Project Team*; *Organizing Projects for Success*; and *Principles of Project Management*.

Managing Projects Step-by-Step

Follow the steps, standards, and procedures used and proven by thousands of professional project managers and leading corporations. This interactive multimedia CD-ROM based on PMI's *A Guide to the Project Management Body of Knowledge*™ will enable you to customize, standardize, and distribute your project plan standards, procedures, and methodology across your entire organization. Multimedia illustrations using 3-D animations and audio make this perfect for both self-paced training or for use by a facilitator.

PMBOK™ Q&A

Use this handy pocket-sized question and answer study guide to learn more about the key themes and concepts presented in PMI's international standard, *A Guide to the Project Management Body of Knowledge*™. More than 160 multiple-choice questions with answers (referenced to the *PMBOK*™ *Guide*) help you with the breadth of knowledge needed to understand key project management concepts.

ISBN: 1-880410-21-4

Project Management Institute Proceedings Library CD-ROM

This interactive guide to PMI's *Annual Seminars & Symposium Proceedings* offers a powerful new option to the traditional methods of document storage and retrieval, research, training, and technical writing. Contains complete paper presentations from PMI '92–PMI '97. Full text search capability, convenient on-screen readability, and PC/Mac compatibility.

Project Management Institute Publications Library CD-ROM

Using state-of-the-art technology, PMI offers complete articles and information from its major publications on one CD-ROM, including *PM Network* (1992–97), *Project Management Journal* (1992–97), and *A Guide to the Project Management Body of Knowledge*™. Offers full text search capability and indexing by *PMBOK*™ *Guide* knowledge areas. Electronic indexing schemes and sophisticated search engines help to find and retrieve articles quickly that are relevant to your topic or research area.

PMI Book of Project Management Forms

More than 150 actual samples and documents, used daily in the management of projects, have been compiled for you to adapt or expand upon. PMI members share forms, checklists, reports, charts, and other sample documents they use in managing their projects to make it easy for practicing project managers or students to get started or to improve their documentation. Spiral bound or CD-ROM formats available.

ISBN: 1-880410-31-1

Also Available from PMI

Principles of Project Management
John Adams et. al.
ISBN: 1-880410-30-3

Organizing Projects for Success
Human Aspects of Project Management Series, Volume 1
Vijay Verma
ISBN: 1-880410-40-0

Human Resource Skills for the Project Manager
Human Aspects of Project Management Series, Volume 2
Vijay Verma
ISBN: 1-880410-41-9

Managing the Project Team
Human Aspects of Project Management Series, Volume 3
Vijay Verma
ISBN: 1-880410-42-7

Earned Value Project Management
Quentin Fleming, Joel Koppelman
ISBN: 1-880410-38-9

Value Management Practice
Michel Thiry
ISBN: 1-880410-14-1

Decision Analysis in Projects
John Schuyler
ISBN: 1-880410-39-7

ABCs of DPC
PMI's Design-Procurement-Construction Specific Interest Group
ISBN: 1-880410-07-9

How to Turn Computer Problems into Competitive Advantage
Tom Ingram
ISBN: 1-880410-08-7

The World's Greatest Project
Russell Darnall
ISBN: 1-880410-46-X

Power & Politics in Project Management
Jeffrey Pinto
ISBN: 1-880410-43-5

Best Practices of Project Management Groups in Large Functional Organizations
Frank Toney, Ray Powers
ISBN: 1-880410-05-2

Send orders to: PMI World Headquarters,
Four Campus Boulevard,
Newtown Square, Pennsylvania, 19073-3299, USA.

Or call 610-356-4600 or fax 610-356-4647.
Order on line at www.pmibookstore.org.